D1134442

BRITISH SALOON CARS

OF THE

EARLY SIXTIES

BRITISH SALOON CARS
OF THE
EARLY SIXTIES

——

MICHAEL ALLEN

First published 1989 by Haynes Publishing Group

© Michael G. D. Allen

This edition published 1995 by
The Promotional Reprint Company
Deacon House, 65 Old Church Street,
Chelsea, London SW3 5BS exclusively for
Bookmart Limited, Desford Road,
Enderby, Leicester LE9 5AD

ISBN 1 85648 254 5

Printed and bound in Hong Kong

CONTENTS

INTRODUCTION & ACKNOWLEDGEMENTS

During the early post-war period, the British motor manufacturers had played a leading role in the nation's recovery from the effects of the six years conflict, with much of the passenger car production throughout the 1950s going to overseas markets, and in so doing establishing places in Britain such as Coventry, Cowley, Dagenham and Luton as major exporting centres.

Inexpensive family saloons were the mainstay, with many all-new post-war models in this category soon appearing under the very familiar names of Austin, Ford, Hillman, Morris, Standard, and Vauxhall, and whose products in the family-car classes I dealt with in *British Family Cars of the Fifties,* the preceding volume to this book. Meeting so well as they did the demands of worldwide markets, these British cars were profitable to such an extent that considerable expansion in respect of new manufacturing facilities was able to take place in Britain throughout the 1950s, with the result that each of the makers aiming at the mass-market was able to widen their range of products quite considerably during the early part of the following decade.

Vauxhall introduced their first small model, the Viva, to complete a very effective small, medium (Victor), and large (Velox) series of cars in the under-£1000 bracket; whilst Ford set about plugging the very noticeable gap which hitherto existed between their small-car offerings like the Anglia, and the very much larger Consul/Zephyr models. The B.M.C.'s attempt at offering something for everyone included running the new Mini and 1100 series of small front wheel drive models alongside the company's established conventional small cars, whilst also now extending their badge-engineering policy to cover almost all of their basic range from the smallest to the largest cars. This was to result in the names Wolseley, Riley, and MG being available rather more down-market than in the previous decade. The Rootes Group, too, extended the badge-engineering theme, and also introduced their first small car onto the market in the shape of the rear engined Hillman Imp. Only Standard-Triumph contracted in so far as low-priced models were concerned, for although replacing the Standard Eight and Ten with the pretty Triumph Herald series, their Standard Vanguard/Ensign replacement (Triumph 2000) was priced to compete rather more up-market alongside such as Rovers, Humber Hawk, etc..

Overall, then, the choice was considerably wider than ever before at the popular end of the market as the 1960s unfolded, and the situation was made all the more attractive by a succession of purchase tax reductions which enabled some large, and quite opulent models to be bought for less than £1000; and this at a time when wages were rising steadily, yet inflation was remaining low.

On the face of it, everything did indeed look rosy, with an ever expanding army of buyers for new British cars. Yet, incredibly, whilst Ford and the other American-owned company, Vauxhall, continued to prosper, the wholly British sector of this great industry was running into the troubles which would, eventually, lead to the extinction of many once-proud names. The reason for that unhappy state of affairs were many, but are of course outside the scope of this book which seeks only to look at the new, and often exciting products being aimed at the lower end of the market by the "big five" concerns as they expanded their ranges whilst also following-up their many successes of the 1950s.

In putting together this second volume dealing with British family cars I have again been fortunate in receiving help from many quarters, and so it is with much gratitude that I record the names which follow: Bob Murray, editor of *Autocar,* and Howard Walker editor of *Motor,* for kindly allowing me to reproduce performance figures taken from their respective magazines; Howard Foottit, for the loan of much old-car literature; Steve Clark and Sheila Knapman, of Ford Photographic Services, for the supply of Ford archive photographs; and also for the supply of photographs, John Charlton, David Williams, Gordon Hewes, Ian Ingham, John Valentine, fellow author Ray Newell, and fellow author/historian Dave Turner, who had the foresight twenty years or so ago to photograph these types of cars when they were still in ordinary use at a time when the large-scale preservation movement which now exists was a long way off; finally, W.G. Elsey, John Evans, and Stephen Rennie, for making their cars available for a session in front of my own camera.

Many thanks indeed to you all.
Michael G.D. Allen.

1

B.M.C.

Although it was a logical, and worthy successor to the popular A30/A35 series, the new A40 announced in September 1958 was for some time an additional model in BMC's range of small cars as the A35 was to continue in production alongside.

The biggest talking point about the new model was its neat Farina-styled bodywork, as this was the first of the whole series of BMC models which would bear the stamp of this well-known Italian styling house. Designed from the outset to include some of the desirable features of an estate car in what was still essentially a small family saloon, the new appearance was characterized by the lack of a separate luggage boot. However, the continuation of a straight-through wing line from the front to slightly beyond the nicely raked rear body line was largely successful in camouflaging the van-like proportions.

To be available only in a two-door configuration, this monocoque body relied partly upon the stressed-skin principle for adequate rigidity, with the transmission tunnel, sills, and vertical heelboard running transversely beneath the rear seat all playing an important part. Additionally under the rear portion were longitudinal U-section members, these running from the heelboard, over the rear axle and continuing to the rear where they gave good side protection to the underslung 6 gallon fuel tank. At the front, lying horizontally, were a pair of pressed steel stiffeners running from beneath the front seat position and terminating at the front panel; two similar vertical stiffeners reinforced each inner wing.

Longer by 8 inches overall, and wider by 4 inches than the A35, whilst being also of appreciably squarer shape, the Farina bodywork offered usefully greater internal dimensions in what was still nevertheless a small car from an external point of view. Very wide doors, and tip-up front seats, ensured easy access to both front and rear. Lying flat behind the rear seat was the spare wheel, complete with a hard cover on which baggage could be safely stowed. Beneath the full-width rear window was an equally wide drop-down tailgate held horizontally by a pair of straps when lowered. This was not however stressed for load carrying, but longer loads than normal for this class of car were catered for by virtue of the estate car type folding rear seat squab. An interior tonneau cover arrangement was provided, so hiding any items being carried in the rear if and when desired.

PVC trim material was used to good effect, with the seating displaying a neat pleated design. The front seats consisted of foam rubber cushioning over a plastic webbing, with the rear seats being of the interior spring type. The painted metal facia included a lidded glove box on the passenger side, and was complete with a padded top covered in black vinyl. A very usefully sized parcel shelf ran full width below the facia panel. The instrument cluster comprised the stylised speedometer and fuel gauge straight from the A35, with these being viewed through a graceful two-spoked steering wheel; warning lights sufficed for additional information. Toggle switchgear was new, and pendant foot pedals were making a welcome first appearance on a small Austin.

Both doors included swivelling quarter windows, but otherwise displayed a marked economy in that the main windows were devoid of winding mechanism, being simply of the balanced drop type. Fixed rear side windows and the lack of a passenger's sunvisor were further evidence of cost cutting, but on the basic model only, with the De Luxe being equipped with twin sunvisors and front-hinged rear side windows. A heater however was an extra cost item on both models.

Externally, a surprise was that both basic and De Luxe cars were finished in dual tones, with the roof panel being painted in black irrespective of the main colour chosen. Chrome plated bumpers, hubcaps, head and sidelamp surrounds, side strips and front grille were a feature of both cars, with the grille showing the wavy horizontal bars which had first appeared on the Austin Cambridge in 1954. Additional bright metal to be seen on the De Luxe only were the stainless steel surrounds for all windows, and a set of chromed bumper overriders.

The wide, rear-hinged bonnet top was not counterbalanced, being held open by a single stay, it gave good accessibility to items requiring routine attention, and when opened revealed the familiar BMC A-series engine. This was the slightly undersquare, 62.9 mm x 76.2 mm, 948 cc overhead valve unit already powering the Austin A35 and Morris Minor 1000, and which in its new A40 application was in a similar state of tune as on the other Austin. With a single Zenith carburettor, and a compression ratio of 8.3:1, the engine produced 34 bhp at 4750 rpm, and 50 lbs/ft of torque at 2000 rpm. The four-speed gearbox and rear axle of 4.55:1 ratio were also from the

A new look for the roads of Britain – the Farina styling as first applied to the B.M.C. Austin A40. 753 BCG is an early 1961-registered car, depicted here when still in regular use during 1970, and looking good for a nine-year old car.

A35, and as the new car was weighing in at around 1 cwt more a slight performance decrease by comparison with the A35 was indicated. This gearbox was without synchromesh on first gear, but had nicely chosen indirect ratios which were selected by an excellent remote type floor mounted gearchange lever.

Attached to the low front end body stiffening members were independent front suspension units of the double wishbone and coil spring variety, with their movement being controlled by lever arm shock absorbers mounted immediately above. Longitudinally mounted leaf springs, and lever arm shock absorbers located the live rear axle. Cam and peg steering gear was employed in line with usual Austin practice, and, like on the A35, with the steering box and track rods situated safely behind the axle line rather than in the relatively unprotected forward position as on larger Austins.

The Lockheed hydro-mechanical braking system in which the front drums were activated hydraulically whilst those at the rear were operated by mechanical links from a remote cylinder was also as on the A35. Much

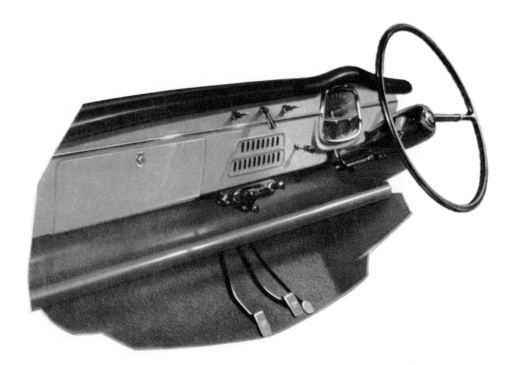

A rather broad expanse of painted metal faced the occupants in the early A40 models, but the overall effect was neat and the instruments were sensibly placed ahead of the driver.

larger front drums however were now fitted, being 8 inches rather than the A35's 7 inches in diameter, and housing wider shoes also than before. This resulted in a total lining area of 76 sq ins, this being more than 20 per cent greater than on the A35. The 13 inch diameter roadwheels retained the 5.20 x 13 tyres which gave overall gearing of 14 mph/1000 rpm with the 4.55:1 axle.

Introduced at £676 and £689 for the basic and De Luxe models, the new car was a hefty £100 or so greater than the corresponding A35 saloons which were continuing for the time being. On the road the A40 was not quite so lively as these, needing as it did some 35 seconds to reach 60 mph, although its ultimate maximum speed of just a little over 70 mph was about the same. Fuel consumption was inevitably somewhat heavier than with the A35, but with 40 mpg at a 50 mph cruising speed the A40 was by no means extragavent in this respect, and it was offering much more convenience in so far as all occupants were concerned, with this being allied also to very modern styling.

Curiously, bearing in mind the A40's rear end design features, it was to be a year before a Countryman estate became available. Consisting simply of the addition now of a lift-up rear window with a self-supporting ratchet type strut, and the provision of a pair of wing mirrors, the Countryman was offered at just £9 more than the De Luxe saloon; this seemed a small price to pay for what was undoubtedly a more versatile model than the fixed window versions.

By this time (October 1959) prices were lower due to purchase tax reductions earlier in the year, and the A40s were now listed at £638 (basic), £650 (De Luxe), and £659 for the Countryman. Already proving very popular, the A40 was now in a stronger position within BMC as the A35 saloons had at last gone, with the new Morris and Austin Mini models coming in at the bottom of the range and not really being in competition with the Farina car. Still unique in its concept, the A40 had no direct rival offering exactly the same amenities, and as it was competitively priced in the small-car market between such as the new Ford 105E Anglia De Luxe

11

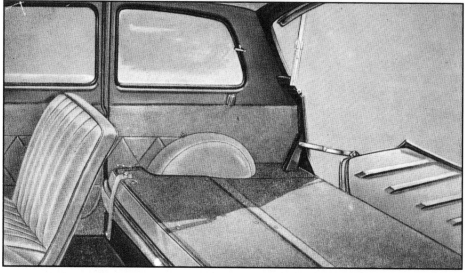

**Interior views show the
four-seat accommodation
applicable to both the
saloon and Countryman
versions, and the useful
stowage space of the
latter when the rear seat
is folded.**

(£610), and the Triumph Herald at £702, its continuing success was assured.

There was some success too in motorsport. In its first Monte Carlo Rally, in January 1959, the A40 had made its mark when Pat Moss and Ann Wisdom won the Ladies Cup with a works prepared car. This result was repeated by the same pairing in the 1960 event, and following this a Don Moore-tuned A40 in the hands of ''Doc'' Shepherd won the BRSCC Touring Car Championship.

After three years of production the A40 went into Mk 2 configuration in October 1961 as the result of a face-lift which also accompanied some under-the-skin improvements. The most obvious change visually was a redesigned grille which was now of plain horizontal bars and extended in width to include the sidelamp/indicator units. A wider colour choice was made available, with single tones now if required and dual schemes in which the roof colour was no longer limited to black. Not quite so obvious at first glance was an increase in the wheelbase of $3^{1}/_{2}$ inches, achieved by placing the rear axle rearwards by that amount along the leaf springs. The overall length remained as before, but the longer wheelbase allowed modifications to the bodyshell in the rear wheelarch area which in turn resulted in the rear seat being placed further back with a consequent improvement in rear compartment kneeroom.

Interior changes also included restyled door and seat trims, in addition to which the doors were now equipped with window winding mechanism in place of the cheaper balanced drop windows. A completely restyled facia faced the driver, and a new self-cancelling indicator stalk on the steering column was a big improvement now over the earlier non-cancelling facia mounted switch.

In this new guise the A40 had actually put on a little weight, but this was being more than compensated for by the adoption of an SU carburettor, mounted on a new one-piece inlet/exhaust manifold, in place of the previous

Datapanel: Austin A40, Mk 2, Mk 2 1100.

	A40 (Mk 2)	Mk2 1100
Engine	4 cyl, ohv	4 cyl, ohv
Capacity	948 cc	1098 cc
Bore	62.9 mm	64.6 mm
Stroke	76.2 mm	83.7 mm
Compresssion ratio	8.3:1	8.3:1
Max BHP	34 nett @ 4750 rpm	47 nett @ 5100 rpm
	(37 nett @ 5000 rpm)	
Max torque	50 lbs/ft @ 2000 rpm	60 lbs/ft @ 2500 rpm
	(50 lbs/ft @ 2500 rpm)	
Gearing	14 mph/1000 rpm	15.3 mph/1000 rpm
Tyres	5.20 x 13	5.20 x 13
Kerb weight	15 cwt (16 cwt)	16 cwt
Overall length	12 ft 1 in	12 ft 1 in
Overall width	4 ft 11 in	4 ft 11 in
Wheelbase	6ft 11$^{1}/_{2}$ in	7 ft 3 in
	(7 ft 3 in)	
Performance		
	"The Motor"	"Autocar"
	R/T No. 9/62	30th November 1962
	Mk 2 948 cc	Mk 2 1100
Max speed		
Top gear	75.2 mph (mean)	78.5 mph (mean)
	79.0 mph (best)	82.5 mph (best)
3rd gear	58 mph	68 mph
2nd gear	34 mph	41 mph
1st gear	–	29 mph
Acceleration		
0–30 mph	6.6 seconds	6.5 seconds
0–50 mph	17.4 seconds	15.7 seconds
0–60 mph	29.0 seconds	23.9 seconds
0–70 mph	45.7 seconds	42.6 seconds
	Top gear/3rd gear	Top gear/3rd gear
20–40 mph	12.9/8.4 seconds	14.9/8.9 seconds
30–50 mph	14.8/10.7 seconds	17.3/9.9 seconds
40–60 mph	21.8/– seconds	17.0/13.7 seconds
50–70 mph	30.0/– seconds	25.7/– seconds
Fuel consumption	34.5 mpg (1280 miles)	30.5 mpg (1116 miles)

Zenith. This change brought the A-series unit into line with that of the Morris Minor 1000 which was still in production, and also resulted in the A40 now acquiring an SU electric fuel pump mounted adjacent to the fuel tank at the rear. The tank capacity was increased slightly now to 7 gallons. An anti-roll bar was added to the front suspension, and at the rear there was a change to telescopic dampers, whilst the hydro-mechanical braking arrangements now gave way to an all hydraulic system.

All of this added up to a much improved A40, with rather more performance than before, and handling qualities in keeping with this improvement. A price increase did accompany these changes, with £694

Announcing the Mk 2 model, this advertisement lists the many improvements incorporated which would keep the A40 competitive. The new full-width grille was the principle Mk 2 recognition feature, and gave the car an appreciably more modern look.

THIS FAMOUS CAR IS NOW EVEN BETTER VALUE

MORE INSIDE AND OUT: The Austin A40 Mk II has advanced in all directions. INSIDE: you experience a new kind of comfort—the roomy back seats allow for the longest legs. A new kind of luxury—restyled trim, new facia panel. OUTSIDE: a completely restyled radiator grille. New carburation gives you more power, greater acceleration. All these new features and the A40 is the same petite overall size, and the price remains as small car as ever.

PRICES. BASIC: £450 plus £169.15.3 Purchase Tax. SUPER DE LUXE: £475 plus £179.2.9 Purchase Tax. EXTRAS ON SUPER DE LUXE INCLUDE: *Fitted carpet throughout. Stainless-steel window surrounds. Bumper over-riders. Passenger sun visor. Windscreen washer. Water temperature gauge.*

NEW Longer wheelbase (3½") gives greater passenger comfort
NEW Anti-roll bar on the front and telescopic rear dampers
NEW Easy-action, wind-down windows
NEW Fully hydraulic brakes on all four wheels
NEW Completely restyled facia with glove box lid/picnic tray
NEW Trafficators that cancel themselves after cornering
NEW Restyled full-width radiator grille
NEW S.U. Carburettor gives increased b.h.p.
NEW Fully-folding rear seat gives more luggage room

Personal Exports Division : 41-46 Piccadilly, London, W.1 · THE AUSTIN MOTOR COMPANY LIMITED · LONGBRIDGE · BIRMINGHAM

NEW AUSTIN A40 MK II

14

now being asked for a De Luxe saloon, but fuel economy remained virtually as before apart from at the top end of the greater speed range.

The A40 continued with this specification for just a year before receiving the 1098 cc development of the A-series engine which was powering the all-new Morris 1100. A slightly larger bore, in conjunction with an appreciably longer stroke, gave the capacity increase, and the 47 bhp at 5100 rpm now being provided indicated a substantial increase in performance. Changes to the transmission consisted of baulk-ring synchromesh in place of the constant load type, and a 4.22:1 axle which now raised the gearing to 15.3 mph/1000 rpm. These changes resulted in a maximum speed of near to 80 mph, and an ability to reach 60 mph from rest in 24 seconds, with only a slight penalty to pay now in increased fuel consumption.

Thanks again to purchase tax reductions, prices had dropped quite considerably earlier in 1962, with the A40 range now being listed at £556 (basic), £599 (De Luxe), £576 (Countryman basic), and £617 for a Countryman with the De Luxe equipment. As a comparison the new Ford Anglia 1200 Super was also at £599. Continuing to sell well, the A40 did not come in for further revision until October 1964, at which time a restyled facia with relocated heater controls appeared. Safety type sunvisors and a safety-framed mirror were also new, along with restyled seating and side trim facings which completed the changes.

Remaining popular despite the more technically advanced cars from its own BMC stable, the A40 continued unchanged before being phased out without a direct replacement during 1967.

A brochure illustration of the A40 Countryman highlights its suitability for countryside pursuits.

AUSTIN CAMBRIDGE A55 MK2, A60, MORRIS OXFORD SERIES V, SERIES VI

Following the merger between Austin and the Nuffield Group of companies in 1952, which resulted in the formation of the British Motor Corporation, came the first examples of rationalisation of common power units throughout. Differing and quite characteristic bodywork would, however, still identify the products as of either Austin or Morris origin. Thus, the BMC's first new releases in the popular $1\frac{1}{2}$ litre category, the Austin Cambridge and Morris Oxford Series III of 1954, had shared what was to be known as the BMC B-Series engine and a common drive line, but otherwise differed completely.

The next stage in rationalisation was to adopt common bodyshells and running gear, just leaving the bright metal external embellishments and alternative interior styling to differentiate between the products of Longbridge (Austin), and the former Morris Motors works at Cowley. This policy was to be seen in the next generation of cars in the important $1\frac{1}{2}$ litre medium-sized family saloon class when, early in 1959 a completely new Austin Cambridge A55 Mk 2, and a Morris Oxford Series V entered production.

As was to be expected, as it followed closely on the heels of the new Austin A40, this new series also exhibited the crisp styling which was a Farina hallmark, and so differed completely from the preceding Cambridge and Oxford models. A straightforward monocoque structure, the new bodyshell was well braced underneath by two full length U-section members welded to the floorpan. At the rear, the wide and quite deep luggage compartment was free of obstruction apart from the rear wheelarches, and had the benefit for loading operations of a wide counterbalanced lid which came down almost to boot floor level. A transverse fuel tank of 10 gallons capacity resided behind the rear seat squab, with a fitted trim panel in the boot hiding it from view. A retractable tray beneath the boot floor housed the sparewheel enabling that item to be reached without disturbing much of the large amount of luggage the new cars were capable of carrying. At the front, the bonnet top had the benefit of a ratchet type self-supporting strut, and was of full width between the prominent front wings.

Four wide doors opened to reveal a passenger compartment of greater room than the preceding Austin Cambridge, but rather smaller than that of the outgoing Morris equivalent. Differing interior trim easily identified the

Still designated A55, but now with a Mk 2 suffix, the new Farina-styled Cambridge bore no outward resemblance to its predecessor. 61 VMC is a well-kept example photographed as recently as 1985.

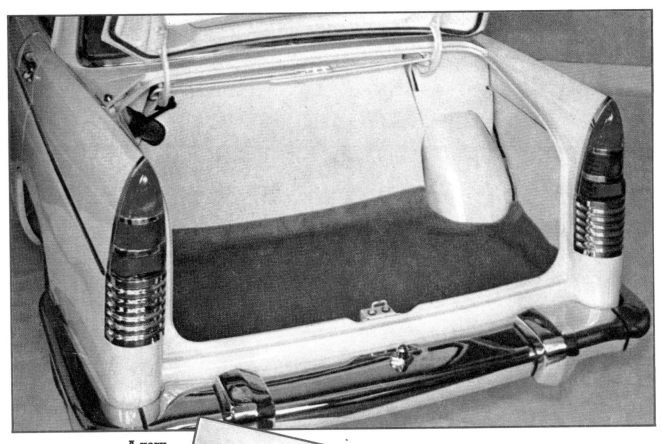

A very
conveniently-shaped, and
easy to load luggage boot
was a good feature of the
1½ litre Farina saloons,
with this illustration
again depicting the
Austin Cambridge.

The facia layout of the
Cambridge, clearly
showing the provision for
the optional radio in the
centre of the panel. The
split-bench front seat was
an already established
Austin feature.

Austin and Morris derivatives, with the former featuring Austin's established split bench front seat, albeit with slightly curved squabs, which could be adjusted together for three-abreast seating. The Oxford displayed a full bench front seat, with a recess centrally in the forward edge of the cushion to allow for the range of movement of the floor mounted gearchange which was a standard fitting on both cars. A wide pull-down central armrest was provided in both front and rear on the Oxford only, which was to be the more expensive of the two cars by a slight amount. Individual front seats could be obtained at extra cost on the Oxford, and a steering column mounted gearchange was a no-cost option which could be specified on both the Austin- and Morris-badged cars.

PVC trim material was to be seen in the basic models, with leather on the wearing surfaces replacing this on the De Luxe cars. The latter also included in their rather better specification such items as a passenger's sunvisor, the heater unit, electric clock, and windscreen washers, for which an extra amount was charged if any of these were required by purchasers of the basic models.

Twin circular instrument housings were immediately in front of the driver, with those of the Oxford being set in a rather more elaborate looking facia panel than the rather plain affair of the Cambridge; the elegant half horn-ring on the Oxford's steering wheel also gave the Morris a more expensive look. In addition to a usefully-sized lidded compartment on the passenger side, was a deep parcel shelf running beneath the facia. The forward edge of the shelf was designed to prevent injury, and both cars featured a safety-padded facia top.

Externally, much use was made of bright metal trim, with a quite liberal use of good quality stainless steel around the the windows, including the door window frames. Substantial, and well-mounted bumpers were chrome plated, and complete with overriders on the De Luxe models. A fine-mesh chrome plated grille identified the Cambridge head-on, whilst that on the Oxford was of horizontal stainless steel bars; each car also had its own exclusive rear lamp clusters for further identification. Two-colour paintwork was to be available at extra cost, with these applications also differing slightly depending upon which car they appeared. The contrasting colour when specified on the Oxford was confined to the roof panel, front screen pillars, and rear quarter pillars only, whereas on the Austin the division was altered to take in the upper half of the boot lid and the prominent tail fins in a most attractive way.

As with the preceding generations, the engine and drive line were being shared, with the well-proven 1489 cc B-Series power unit continuing almost unchanged in respect of its power output. Both models now featured a single SU carburettor, whereas previously a Zenith instrument had appeared on the Austin Cambridge. The compression ratio was 8.3:1, and power and torque outputs were 53 bhp (nett) at 4400 rpm, and 82.5 lbs/ft at 2100 rpm. Well known for its reliability and durable nature, this rugged four-cylinder unit did have a tendency to consume large quantities of lubricating oil if held at high rpm for lengthy periods, and in view of the coming motorway network which would encourage just such usage, piston rings of improved design were introduced into the specification of these latest B-series units. These were a chrome plated top piston ring which would lead to reduced bore wear in the longer term, and a redesigned scraper ring with greater oil-control properties.

The four-speed gearbox was still devoid of synchromesh on bottom gear, but relatively low overall gearing anyway rendered first gear superfluous apart from moving off from rest. The new remote type floor gearchange was

A different grille and hubcaps were amongst the features which identified the Farina Morris Oxford which was now designated Oxford Series V. A 1961 model, 7110 AT is depicted here when ten years old.

to earn much praise for its accuracy. A 4.55:1 axle ratio was new to both cars, giving 15.6 mph/1000 rpm on top gear which was very slightly lower than the previous Cambridge (15.8 mph/1000 rpm), whilst being usefully higher than the previous Oxford's 15 mph/1000 rpm.

The running gear was substantially that of the previous Austin, with the coil and wishbone independent front suspension, and the longitudinal leaf spring arrangements at the rear being stiffened up slightly to cater for approx $1\frac{1}{2}$ cwt increase in kerb weight by comparison with the outgoing Cambridge. Armstrong dampers of the lever-arm type completed the suspension. Cam and lever steering gear was employed, with the steering box, steering arms, and track rods being in a somewhat vulnerable position ahead of the axle line.

In so far as enthusiasts of the earlier Morris Oxfords were concerned, these front end arrangements were seen as a retrograde step when compared with the former Morris product's torsion bar front suspension and rack and pinion steering gear which had earned past Morris Oxfords an excellent reputation for precise control, and which could not be matched by the set up being adopted now.

The Girling hydraulic braking system comprised 9 inch diameter drums all round, with those at the front of increased width by comparison with the previous Cambridge, and so increasing the total lining area from 121 square inches to the very ample figure now of 147 square inches. The improvement here was even more marked in respect of the Oxford, of which the earlier model had made do with a decidedly modest 99 square inches of total lining area.

Introduced at £848 and £876 in Cambridge basic and De Luxe configurations, with £864 and £894 being asked for the corresponding Morris variations, these newcomers were offering sound value which quickly attracted them to an even wider following than their popular predecessors. A high standard of finish was evident throughout, and on the road a maximum speed in excess of 75 mph was coupled with an ability to reach 60 mph from rest in 25 seconds. Excellent top gear flexibility was a strong

At the rear, a slightly different tail lamp treatment accompanied the Morris Oxford badge. This contemporary brochure illustration captures the prominence of the tail fins on these early Farina cars.

A front bench seat was to be found inside the Oxford, but the close proximity of the gearlever still made three-abreast seating rather difficult in the front. The chromed hornring adds a touch of class by comparison with the Cambridge.

point also, and fuel consumption figures in the 30 to 35 mpg range were within easy reach, whilst riding qualities at touring speeds were usually judged to be good for this class of car. The rear seating was criticised by some as the curved backrest (to clear slight wheelarch intrusion) forced occupants to face slightly inwards, and so discouraged three-abreast seating by large adults. Likewise, the "press-on" types of driver were discouraged somewhat by the imprecise steering and rather wallowy cornering characteristics. But these were essentially family cars, and their overall roominess and convenience, economy, nice finish and trouble-free nature endeared them to many people.

Estate car versions appeared at the Earls Court Motor Show in October 1960, known as the A55 Countryman and Morris Oxford Traveller, as had been previous generations of Austin and Morris estate cars of so many types. Although retaining the saloon's rear wings complete with the prominent fins, the estate cars differed considerably from the saloons from the centre pillar rearwards. Rear passenger doors now with squared up window frames were fitted, and there was a full size rear window aft of these; the rear pillars were raked sufficiently to give a nice appearance. At the rear was a horizontally-split tailgate, with the upper half consisting of a full width window, and being self-supporting when open with a ratchet type strut. A tip-forward rear seat cushion, and fold-flat squab were provided, and with the addition of an over-centre arrangement which allowed the folded seat to lie further forward if the front seats were moved to the fully forward position of their adjustment. With everything thus, a comfortable sleeping length was provided in the rear.

Stronger rear springs were fitted, in conjunction with larger (6.40 x 14) tyres with which to cater for the heavier loads. An anti-roll bar was introduced into the rear suspension in order to reduce any swaying tendencies with a fully laden rear. Even unladen, the state cars weighed an additional $1\frac{1}{2}$ cwt, and so easing the engine's job was a lower axle ratio of 4.875:1 which, even allowing for the larger tyres, reduced the overall gearing to 15 mph/1000 rpm. At £914 and £929 for the Austin and Morris versions, respectively, these estate cars were attractive load carriers which retained all the normal saloon car ammenities.

Considerably revised Cambridge and Oxford models appeared for the Motor Show in October 1961, with designations now of A60, and Oxford Series VI. A larger capacity development of the B-series power unit was of 1622 cc, with this being arrived at by an increase in bore size now to 76.2 mm. The compression ratio remained as before at 8.3:1, but slightly larger valves were now employed. The power and torque outputs showed a useful increase with 61 bhp (nett) at 4500 rpm and 90 lbs/ft at 2100 rpm, and to cope with this increase came an improved crankshaft and connecting rods. Raised overall gearing accompanied the larger engine, this being achieved with a 4.3:1 axle ratio which gave 16.6 mph/1000 rpm. The saloon's former 4.55:1 axle was continued now for the estate cars, thus raising their gearing slightly.

A most welcome improvement was much better stability now by the introduction of anti-roll bars at both front and rear along with increasing the front track measurement by two inches, and that at the rear by $1\frac{1}{4}$ inches. A 1 inch longer wheelbase was arrived at by relocating the rear axle further aft along the leaf springs by that amount, and this change in conjunction with the wider rear track allowed the provision of an improved rear seat better able to accomodate three persons. Other internal changes were improved switchgear, and on the Austin a restyled facia which in fact was still in metal, but had a very realistic-looking walnut finish.

21

660HFC

OUR 60

Getting ready for the
seaside. A lovely
brochure illustration of
the new A60 Cambridge
which appeared for 1962.

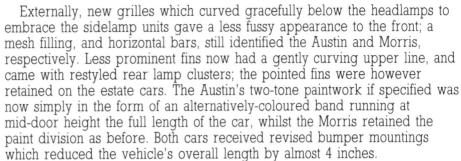

Externally, new grilles which curved gracefully below the headlamps to embrace the sidelamp units gave a less fussy appearance to the front; a mesh filling, and horizontal bars, still identified the Austin and Morris, respectively. Less prominent fins now had a gently curving upper line, and came with restyled rear lamp clusters; the pointed fins were however retained on the estate cars. The Austin's two-tone paintwork if specified was now simply in the form of an alternatively-coloured band running at mid-door height the full length of the car, whilst the Morris retained the paint division as before. Both cars received revised bumper mountings which reduced the vehicle's overall length by almost 4 inches.

An interesting new option was a fully automatic gearbox, this being the new Borg Warner Model 35, which included a manual "lock up" override facility for low and intermediate gear. The Model 35 was a substantially more compact and lighter unit than the Borg Warner DG gearbox which had only been suitable for large-engined cars, and in the Cambridge/Oxford installation the new gearbox proved to have little adverse effect upon either speed or acceleration, and was an attractive "extra" at £100.

In this latest guise, the Cambridge and Oxford were much improved cars. There was usefully more performance now, with a maximum speed of 80 mph and livelier acceleration than before, and with handling qualities now that whilst not in the sports-saloon category were however rather more in keeping with the performance on offer. With £884 and £898 being asked for the De Luxe versions of the Cambridge and Oxford, the BMC twins did have stiff competition to face from such as the Vauxhall Victor De Luxe (£847), and the Hillman Super Minx at £854, both of which were new releases. Nevertheless, the Austin/Morris cars continued to appeal greatly to many motorists who favoured a conservative approach to car styling and design, and who appreciated a well-developed concept of equally well-proven dependability.

The overall design was now well and truly frozen, and only very slight detail changes took place over the ensuing years. These included, in 1962, lower rear spring rates and the standardisation of two tone paintwork on the Austin, and in late 1964 improved steering box mounting and the provision of safety type crushable sunvisors. Purchase tax reductions during 1962, and the fact that there were no further development costs to absorb would now keep the Cambridge/Oxford duo competitively priced, and in spite of much newer opposition from elsewhere and within BMC, their sales were such as to justify continued production. In fact it was not until 1969 that the Cambridge was phased out, leaving the Oxford to soldier on into 1971 before it too was deleted.

The upmarket badge-engineered derivatives

Running concurrently with the "bread-and-butter" Cambridge and Oxford models were the appreciably more upmarket badge-engineered versions under the Wolseley, MG, and Riley marque names. These shared the same engines, transmissions, and running gear as the Cambridge/Oxford cars, but with the important difference that on the MG and Riley derivatives the engine was in a higher state of tune appropriate to the sporting history of these two marques, and that with these tuned units came the 4.3:1 axle ratio from the start.

The first of these to appear, actually preceding the Austin by a month or so, was the Wolseley 15/60, complete with a traditional Wolseley grille neatly grafted into the modern Farina bodywork which was otherwise identical to the downmarket Austin/Morris cars. Its performance and road

23

The Oxford became Series VI also for 1962, and here, pictured in 1988, the beautifully-preserved DWX 275B displays the model's extensive bright metal embellishments to good effect in the twilight of a summer evening.

manners too were of course identical, but inside it was quite lavishly equipped in the Wolseley tradition. Polished wood facia and door cappings, real leather upholstery, and deep pile carpeting were provided, and along with such items as the heater and windscreen washers as standard equipment at a time when these were still definitely an "extra" on more cars than not.

An MG Magnette 111, and a Riley 4/68 quickly followed, with the latter's designation indicating that these two versions featured a 68 bhp version of the B-series engine. Twin SU carburettors, and a modified exhaust system were responsible for the increased power output, and enabled the MG and Riley to reach 60 mph from rest in around 21 seconds whilst on their way to a maximum speed approaching 85 mph.

Like the Wolseley, these two featured their own individual grilles of upright design which reflected an earlier era. Additionally, the MG and Riley could be identified from the rear by their cut-back fins which, in the opinion of many, gave a far better visual balance to this Farina line than did the pointed fins of the others in the series. Here again the trim was carried out in the more expensive materials, and a neat touch in the MG was the continuing link with the past in the half octagon-shaped speedometer which faced the driver. An additional instrument found only in the Riley was a nice circular rev-counter to match its speedometer.

The larger engines, improved suspension, and the wheelbase and track increases introduced in October 1961 resulted in these cars now becoming known as the Wolseley 16/60, MG Magnette IV, and Riley 4/72. Because of

Datapanel: Austin Cambridge A55, A60. Morris Oxford Series V, Series VI.

	A55/Series V	A60/Series VI
Engine	4 cyl, ohv	4 cyl, ohv
Capacity	1498 cc	1622 cc
Bore	73 mm	76.2 mm
Stroke	88.9 mm	88.9 mm
Compression ratio	8.3:1	8.3:1
Max BHP	53 nett @ 4400 rpm	61 nett @ 4500 rpm
Max torque	82.5 lbs/ft @ 2100 rpm	90 lbs/ft @ 2100 rpm
Gearing	15.6 mph/1000 rpm	16.6 mph/1000 rpm
Tyres	5.90 x 14	5.90 x 14
Kerb weight	$21^1/2$ cwt	$21^1/2$ cwt
Overall length	14 ft $10^1/2$ in	14 ft $6^1/2$ in
Overall width	5 ft $3^1/2$ in	5 ft $3^1/2$ in
Wheelbase	8ft $3^1/4$ in	8 ft $4^1/4$ in
Performance		
	"The Motor" R/T No. 16/60	"Autocar" 6th April 1962
Max speed		
Top gear	78.3 mph (mean) 80.4 mph (best)	80.7mph (mean) 84.0 mph (best)
3rd gear	62 mph	70 mph
2nd gear	42 mph	44 mph
1st gear	24 mph	26 mph
Acceleration		
0–30 mph	6.6 seconds	5.8 seconds
0–50 mph	16.6 seconds	14.6 seconds
0–60 mph	25.4 seconds	21.4 seconds
0–70 mph	39.3 seconds	29.7 seconds
	Top gear/3rd gear	Top gear/3rd gear
20–40 mph	11.6/8.4 seconds	9.9/7.6 seconds
30–50 mph	12.6/9.8 seconds	11.2/8.6 seconds
40–60 mph	15.7/14.2 seconds	13.7/11.5 seconds
50–70 mph	25.0/– seconds	15.1/18.2 seconds
Fuel consumption	26.2 mpg (1065 miles)	26.2 mpg (1389 miles)

their protruding bonnet fronts these cars did not get the revised bumper mountings of the Austin and Morris models, and so remained the same overall length as before. The Wolseley did receive the lower fins, but the MG and Riley continued with their cut-back version of the earlier fins.

Always selling at prices some 20 to 25 per cent higher than the Oxford and Cambridge, these badge-engineered luxury versions were never in the top value-for-money stakes. Even so, they did have a small following which was sufficient enough to warrant BMC keeping them in production alongside the cheaper mass-market models before first the MG, and then the Riley were deleted in the late 1960s, leaving the Wolseley to continue alongside the Morris Oxford until the demise of the series in 1971.

Always mechanically identical to the Austin/Morris versions, the Farina Wolseley also featured similar rear end bodywork treatment, whereas . . .

PASSPORT . . . TWO WEEKS . . . WOLSELEY 15 60

There's something special about a Wolseley 15/60 holiday. Perhaps it's the brisk acceleration and effortless high cruising speed. Or the unrestricted 4/5 seater luxury that makes every mile a joy. Or could it be the money you save on petrol. More probably it's a combination of all three. 1½ litre O.H.V. engine. 4-speed gearbox. Central floor gear change. Panoramic vision and a host of luxury features. From £660 plus £276.2.6 P.T. (incl. heater).

BUY WISELY —BUY WOLSELEY
TWELVE MONTHS' WARRANTY and backed by BMC service

26

For the man who really cares

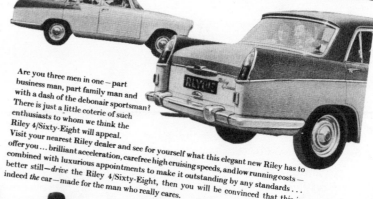

Are you three men in one — part business man, part family man and with a dash of the debonair sportsman? There is just a little coterie of such enthusiasts to whom we think the Riley 4/Sixty-Eight will appeal. Visit your nearest Riley dealer and see for yourself what this elegant new Riley has to offer you ... brilliant acceleration, carefree high cruising speeds, and low running costs — combined with luxurious appointments to make it outstanding by any standards ... better still — *drive* the Riley 4/Sixty-Eight, then you will be convinced that this is indeed *the* car — made for the man who really cares.

Price **£725** *plus £303.4.2 P.T. Duotone colours extra.*

BMC

Every RILEY *carries a 12 months' WARRANTY and is backed by Europe's most comprehensive service — B.M.C.*

Riley **4 SIXTY EIGHT**

for pace and prestige

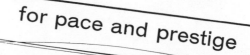

Extra pace, readily available, is but one of a score of plus features which give the M.G. Magnette Mark III its special place among today's fine cars. With its "safety fast" tradition, it appeals to the owner who not only likes to move rapidly when it is safe to do so, but who prides himself on always driving with skill and polish. For such drivers, this thoroughbred sports saloon is a constant joy to handle, its twin carburetter engine providing sparkling third gear acceleration and really economical high speed cruising in top. Ask for a demonstration run.

Price £714.0.0 plus £298.12.6 P.T. Duotone colours extra.

MG *Safety fast!*

. . . not only were the MG and Riley variants rather more powerful, as they also featured a different rear fin treatment as shown here in the Riley advertisement.

AUSTIN WESTMINSTER A99, A110, A110 MK2

The third model in BMC's Farina-styled series was announced in August 1959, this being the new Austin Westminster A99, to replace the existing A95 and A105 Westminster models.

Based upon a 2 inch greater wheelbase (9 ft) than the earlier car, the appreciably larger bodywork carried the Farina characteristics particularly well, with the somewhat restrained fins (by comparison with the BMC 1½ litre models) achieving a more harmonious line for what was overall an impressive looking car. The base of the monocoque structure was a very substantially built floorpan made up of several sections. Further stiffening was by longitudinal U-section members welded to the underside inboard of the sill area at either side, and running the full length of the car.

Beneath the very wide, flat boot floor length was a retractable sparewheel housing, and a 16 gallon fuel tank resided transversely in the luggage compartment behind the rear seat squab; a flat shelf above the tank gave useful additional stowage for smaller soft items of baggage. Spring loaded and self-supporting when open, the bootlid had the added convenience of

opening from almost the compartment floor level.

Zero-torque locks which avoided the need for any slamming were a feature of the four passenger compartment doors, each of which also being equipped with opening quarter windows and a chromed doorpull; a padded armrest appeared on all but the driver's door. Front seats of the split bench type, allowing six-seater accommodation when required, were in keeping with Austin practice, with each side of the bench having its own adjustment and a folding armrest. A pull-down centre armrest was provided in the rear, and leather coverings on all seat's wearing surfaces helped towards a quality feel as did deep pile carpeting throughout. The roof lining was in a light-coloured washable plastic-coated material. A rather plain, painted metal facia panel seemed a little out of character with the rest of the interior, although it did feature a padded top which also formed a slight lip.

The large, and deeply dished steering wheel, was complete with a lower half hornring which sounded twin windtone instruments. Twin circular dials flanked the steering column, with that containing the speedometer being matched by one housing the respective gauges for fuel, engine temperature, and oil pressure. An electric clock occupied a central position in the upper half of the facia panel, whilst beneath this was provision for the optional radio. A lidded compartment faced the passenger seat, with other stowage space being provided by a shelf running beneath the facia panel, although its centre portion was occupied by the heating and demisting equipment which was a standard fitting. Two-speed electric windscreen wipers, and a vacuum operated windscreen washer were also standard.

Single or dual tone exterior paintwork could be specified, with this being highlighted by considerable bright metal trim, of which the very substantial, chrome plated bumpers featured overriders as standard equipment.

Weighing in at 30 cwt unladen, the A99 was heavier than its predecessor by some $3\frac{1}{4}$ cwt, but more than compensating for this was an increased capacity version of BMC's reliable C-Series six-cylinder engine. Whilst the stroke remained the same at 88.9 mm, a greater bore diameter now of 83.34 mm (79.4 mm previously) resulted in a capacity increase from 2639 cc to 2912 cc for this latest car. Achieving this had meant 'siamezing' bores 1 and 2, 3 and 4, and 5 and 6, with water jacketing now simply around each of these pairs rather than every individual cylinder as in the earlier unit. A gear type oil pump in place of the previous engine's eccentric lobe type,

Surprisingly, the mandatory rear reflectors appear to have been only included as an afterthought on the otherwise impeccably-styled Westminster.

Slight changes to the grille and headlamp treatment identified the more powerful A110. Glamour and style are once again emphasised in this brochure illustration. Cars such as the Westminster certainly had a "presence" which somehow never seems to be the case with today's wind-tunnel-wonders.

Another page from the brochure highlights the practical rear end layout.

The rear compartment of the A110 Westminster holds a huge amount of family luggage, and has a spring-balanced lid for easy lifting. The floor is neatly covered with vinyl-treated felt and is illuminated at night by the rear number plate lamp. Prominently mounted at the rear are the combined stop/tail lamps and flashing direction indicators. This ensures that a clear indication of the driver's intention is given to following traffic. Night driving presents no problems, for powerful double-dipping headlamps — hooded to reduce back glare—brilliantly illuminate the road ahead.

A major contribution to the roominess of the luggage compartment is the carrying of the spare wheel in a special tray beneath the boot floor. The tray is completely weatherproof and can be lowered by means of the starting handle.

30

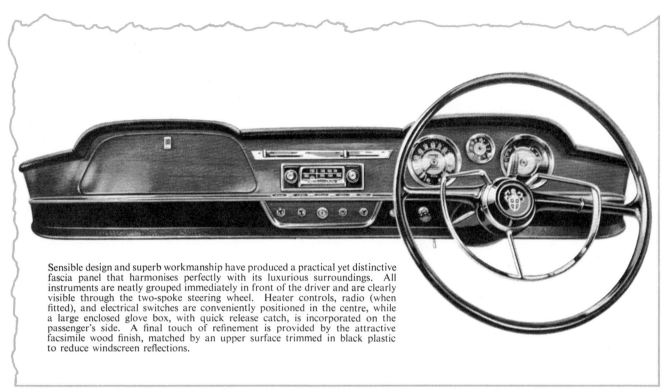

Sensible design and superb workmanship have produced a practical yet distinctive fascia panel that harmonises perfectly with its luxurious surroundings. All instruments are neatly grouped immediately in front of the driver and are clearly visible through the two-spoke steering wheel. Heater controls, radio (when fitted), and electrical switches are conveniently positioned in the centre, while a large enclosed glove box, with quick release catch, is incorporated on the passenger's side. A final touch of refinement is provided by the attractive facsimile wood finish, matched by an upper surface trimmed in black plastic to reduce windscreen reflections.

Well placed instruments faced the driver, but the centrally mounted switches would not seem to be quite so conveniently situated as the brochure caption suggests.

and a four-bladed rather than two-bladed cooling fan were other changes.

The new cylinder head gave a similar 8.3:1 compression ratio as before, and twin SU carburettors were standard. These were fed by two SU electric fuel pumps mounted close to the tank in the rear of the car; failure of one of these pumps would still leave the car driveable, but only up to about a two thirds throttle opening. The maximum bhp was 102.5 nett at 4500 rpm, with a hefty 158 lbs/ft of torque at just 2000 rpm suggesting excellent flexibility.

The 10 inch diameter clutch was hydraulically operated as before, but there was now an entirely new gearbox. This was an all synchromesh three-speed unit, with the synchromesh mechanism being of the Porsche type with a spring-steel synchroniser ring, thrust block, anchor block and brake bands. A steering column gearchange lever was provided, and chamfered teeth on the plain reverse gear aided engagement of that ratio. Supplementing the gearbox was the well known Borg Warner overdrive as standard equipment, operating on any gear above about 30 mph, and so for practical purposes in this particular application on second and top gear. The usual Borg Warner kick-down disengagement, and freewheeling facility below 30 mph if required, were provided. When engaged, the overdrive gave a 30 per cent reduction in engine rpm for any given road speed. A hypoid bevel final drive assembly with a ratio of 3.91:1 gave 19 mph/1000 rpm in direct top gear, and a usefully long-legged 27 mph/1000 rpm in overdrive.

An alternative transmission at extra cost was the Borg Warner Model DG fully automatic. A manual intermediate gear "hold" was provided in this Austin installation in addition to the usual low-gear hold facility. When equipped with this transmission the Westminster came with a revised axle ratio of 3.55:1, this giving 20.9 mph/1000 rpm in top gear.

Conventional independent front suspension comprised coil springs and upper and lower wishbones, whilst the non-independent rear featured a pair of longitudinally mounted half-elliptic leaf springs. Armstrong lever arm shock absorbers, and an anti-roll bar at both the front and rear completed the Westminster's suspension. At the front the suspension units were carried by a box-section crossmember, with rubber insulators at the four body mounting points. Operated by a variable ratio cam and lever type steering box, mounted ahead of the axle line, was a three-piece track rod arrangement linked to forward-facing steering arms.

Well able to cope with the new Westminster's performance potential was a new Lockheed servo-assisted hydraulic braking system, with disc brakes at the front making their first appearance on an Austin family saloon. These were 10.8 inches in diameter, and were in conjunction with 10 inch diameter rear drums housing shoes of 3 inch width. A pressure-limiting valve in the hydraulic line to the rear brakes allowed emergency stops to be made without rear wheel locking. Completing the running gear came 14 inch diameter roadwheels equipped with 7.00 x 14 Dunlop Gold Seal crossply tyres.

Being listed at £1148, the new Westminster was actually priced at £19 less than the outgoing Westminster A105, but was still somewhat more expensive than its two main rivals in the six-cylinder family class. These were the well established Ford Zodiac Mk 2 (£957) and Vauxhall Cresta PA at £1014. However, neither of these had the advantage at this time of a power-assisted disc brake set up, and as in both cases the overdrive was only available at an extra cost of some £65, the big Austin could certainly be seen as sound value for money. With an ability to reach 60 and 70 mph in 16 and 25 seconds, the Austin could slightly out-accelerate the rival Ford and Vauxhall models, and continue to a considerably higher maximum speed of around 97 mph. Being appreciably heavier than these however, its fuel consumption at around 17 to 18 mpg overall was the poorer by some 4 or 5 mpg.

Criticism regarding an engine vibration at near peak rpm on some of the earliest production models was quickly attended to with the introduction of a stiffer bell housing, and the Westminster settled down to a production run of just over two years before significant changes in the specification were made in September 1961, at which time the car was redesignated A110.

Cylinder head modifications, a reprofiled camshaft, and a dual exhaust system combined to raise the power output to 120 bhp at 4750 rpm, with a correspondingly useful increase in the maximum torque also, this now being 163 lbs/ft at 2750 rpm. A floor mounted gearchange lever replaced the column change of the A99. This latest Westminster also rode on a 2 inch greater wheelbase, as the rear axle had been repositioned further back along the springs by that amount. A transverse telescopic damper between the axle and bodyshell was now introduced as additional rear axle location.

The lengthened wheelbase allowed redesigned rear wheelarches and the provision of improved rear seating, whilst another internal change visible was the adoption of a wood-grain finish for the facia panel. Externally, a redesigned and rather plainer grille, and oblong rather than the previous circular front sidelamp/flasher assemblies were the A110 identification features. The price was now £1269, at which the Westminster was offering improvements in both riding qualities and performance, with the latter now including a genuine 100 mph capability. A purchase tax reduction in April 1962 brought the Westminster down to £1197, at which price it was comparing only slightly unfavourably with Ford's new Mk 3 Zodiac at £1070.

Apart from the availability of power-assisted steering which became an extra-cost option during 1962, and the introduction of an automatically operated luggage boot interior light late in 1963, the Westminster now continued unchanged until the announcement of the A110 Mk 2 in May 1964.

Now to be available in both basic and Super De Luxe configuration, this revised Westminster was fundamentally the same car as before, but nevertheless incorporating sufficient technical and trim changes to warrant

the Mk 2 label. A redesigned single exhaust system, incorporating three silencers, replaced the twin system of the previous car but with no change in the quoted power and torque outputs. A new Borg & Beck diaphragm type clutch was fitted, and behind this now was the four-speed gearbox from the Austin Healey 3000, and which had already been fitted to some BMC C-Series saloon police cars. This was devoid of synchromesh on bottom gear, and was replacing the standard all synchromesh three-speed and overdrive arrangement, with the overdrive however still being available as an optional extra. A transmission change for the automatic model also was to be seen in the adoption of the new, and lighter in weight, Borg Warner Model 35 fully automatic gearbox.

Considerable suspension changes took place at the rear. Here the leaf springs were lengthened by 4 inches, and a pair of inward-angled telescopic shock absorbers now replaced the two lever arm, and one transverse telescopic damping arrangements, the body also now sat lower on the suspension by just over a $1/2$ inch. Thicker front brake discs, and self-adjusting rear drums were in conjunction with a more powerful Lockheed servo than before, and a further running gear modification was the adoption of 13 inch diameter roadwheels. The latter were now shod with 7.50 x 13 tyres, thus maintaining the same overall gearing as with the previous 7.00 x 14 set up, but now saving a useful 10 lbs weight per wheel.

PVC upholstery, the deletion of the armrests and the facia clock, and the lack of overriders were economies which identified the new basic Westminster, but which had allowed the tax-paid price to fall slightly below the £1000 barrier, with just £997 in fact being asked for this still impressive Austin. For those buyers wishing for a little luxury now was the Super De Luxe. Leather upholstery, walnut veneered facia with its own strip speedometer, walnut doorcappings and a walnut finish to rear compartment

Datapanel: Austin Westminster A99 A110 A110 Mk 2

	A99	A110 (Mk 2)
Engine	6 cyl, ohv	6 cyl, ohv
Capacity	2912 cc	2912 cc
Bore	83.3 mm	83.3 mm
Stroke	88.9 mm	88.9 mm
Compression ratio	8.3:1	8.3:1
Max BHP	102.5 @ 4500 rpm	120 @ 4750 rpm
Max torque	158 lbs/ft @ 2000 rpm	163 lbs/ft @ 2750 rpm
Gearing	19 mph/1000 rpm	19 mph/1000 rpm
Tyres	7.00 x 14	7.00 x 14 (7.50 x 13)
Kerb weight	30 cwt	30 cwt (28 $\frac{1}{2}$ cwt)
Overall length	15 ft 8 in	15 ft 8 in
Overall width	5 ft 8$\frac{1}{2}$ in	5 ft 8$\frac{1}{2}$ in
Wheelbase	9 ft	9 ft 2 in
Performance		
	"The Autocar" 25th September 1959	"Autocar" 10th July 1964 A110 Mk 2
Max speed		
O/D	97.6 mph (mean) 98.0 mph (best)	– –
Top gear	94.3 mph (mean) 95.0 mph (best)	100.8 mph (mean) 102.0 mph (best)
O/D 2nd	84 mph	81 mph (3rd gear)
2nd gear	65 mph	51 mph
1st gear	36 mph	40 mph
Acceleration		
0–30 mph	4.9 seconds	5.0 seconds
0–50 mph	12.1 seconds	11.9 seconds
0–60 mph	15.8 seconds	16.2 seconds
0–70 mph	22.9 seconds	21.2 seconds
0–80 mph	33.3 seconds	29.1 seconds
	Top gear/2nd gear	Top gear/3rd gear
20–40 mph	10.0/5.7 seconds	9.2/6.7 seconds
30–50 mph	9.9/6.3 seconds	8.9/7.1 seconds
40–60 mph	10.6/8.0 seconds	10.0/7.6 seconds
50–70 mph	11.9/10.7 seconds (O/D 2nd)	11.6/9.0 seconds
60–80 mph	13.5/12.6 seconds (O/D 2nd)	13.2/11.9 seconds
Fuel consumption	17.3 mpg (1373 miles)	17.9 mpg (998 miles)

13 inch diameter wheels and huge crossply tyres identify the A110 Mk 2. Registered in 1966, GAT 736D is a Super De Luxe Westminster pictured when a mere five years old.

picnic tables, padded door armrests with built in pockets, and fully reclining front seat backs were the principle features accounting for the £1112 price tag of this variant, at which price it still represented excellent value.

A slightly cheapened De Luxe car, devoid of the walnut trimmings and picnic tables, appeared early in 1965, slotting in nicely between the basic and Super De Luxe cars. However, this version apparently only served to complicate the range somewhat, and it was discontinued a year or so later, thus leaving the established basic and Super De Luxe cars in production. These two versions remained as Austin's contenders in the six-cylinder family car market until early in 1968 when replaced by the completely new Austin 3 litre which inherited nothing from the big Farina models.

AUSTIN SEVEN/MORRIS MINI MINOR MK1 MODELS & DERIVATIVES

The typical British post-war small family car, and indeed many from an earlier period, had generally displayed the proportions and overall appearance of much larger cars. This was due in part to following closely the established, conventional mechanical layout for passenger saloons, and at the same time retaining styling features more appropriate to the larger models.

A watercooled power unit, with its cylinders in line and the cooling-water radiator ahead required quite considerable space; whilst relatively thick doors, a nicely raked windscreen, and curving roofline, all of which were fine on a $5^1/2$ feet wide and 15 feet long car, imposed serious restrictions on interior space in a car narrower by only 3 or 4 inches, and shorter by 2 or 3 feet. Therefore, despite having designed the big-selling and much loved Morris Minor, itself today widely regarded as a classic amongst small cars, Alex Issigonis abandoned convention completely for his next economy-car design. This was to appear in August 1959 as the B.M.C.'s Austin Seven and Morris Mini Minor, and subsequently prove to be arguably

**An impressive
double-page spread was
chosen by Morris to
announce the Mini-Minor,
and showing many of the
interesting details of what
was then a revolutionary
car.**

the most significant small car in post-war motoring history.

By adopting a front wheel drive layout, and also mounting the engine
transversely across the engine compartment, the length of that compartment
was reduced to something like half that of the bonnet of even very small
cars with conventionally-mounted power units. It was not even necessary to
design a completely new engine, as the well-proven A-Series four-cylinder
unit proved readily adaptable to this new layout, and was short enough to fit
snugly between the inner front wings of what was quite a narrow car.

The same cylinder block as on the 948 cc Morris Minor and Austin A35
was used, and with the same 62.9 mm bore. But with a new crankshaft of
shorter throw reducing the stroke from 76.2 mm to 68.26 mm, the swept
volume was now down to 848 cc. The compression ratio was 8.3:1, and with
a single SU carburettor 34 bhp and 44 lbs/ft torque were developed at a
relatively high 5500 rpm and 2900 rpm, respectively. What would normally
be the front of the engine was now at the nearside (left) and here was to be
found the usual belt-driven fan and a radiator squeezed in between the
engine and the inner wing. The fan was of opposite to normal pitch, and
drew air in through the grille situated across the front of the car and
pushed this air through the radiator and out of the engine compartment
through outlets in the inner wing. The crankshaft featured an extension at its
rear on which was a free-running gearwheel toothed around one side only
and lipped at the other. Around this gearwheel, centrally between the

**A clever Austin
advertisement
emphasizes the
four-seater
accommodation of Alec
Issigonis's brainchild.**

Unique in 1959, but commonplace amongst small cars today, the transverse engine layout of the BMC Mini. The wavy grille bars just visible identify this as an Austin Mini.

toothed and lipped sides was the clutch plate, with the whole of this assembly being inboard of the flywheel. When the clutch was engaged the toothed end of the gearwheel was brought into mesh with an idler gear beneath, transferring the drive downwards through this to the main driving gear of the transmission assembly.

The whole gearbox and final-drive assembly was situated immediately beneath the crankshaft in an appropriately enlarged sump, and was therefore sharing a common oil supply. Four forward speeds were provided, utilising much from the existing A-series gearbox including the constant-load synchromesh between the upper three ratios. The differential and final-drive gears were at the rear of the package as installed, from where the power was transmitted to the front wheels via short drive shafts. At the inboard end of each of these was a universal joint and splined sliding coupling, whilst at the outboard end was the complex constant-velocity joint necessary to transmit power to the steerable wheels. The rather high final drive ratio of 3.76:1 was in conjunction with roadwheels of only 10 inch diameter, shod with 5.20 x 10 tyres, with the result being overall gearing of 14.9 mph/1000 rpm.

The whole engine/transmission package was amazingly compact, and was mounted on a sturdy little subframe which also housed the neat suspension and steering arrangements. The independent front suspension used an upper and lower wishbone layout but was novel in that compressible rubber units were replacing the more usual coil springs. These rubber units had been developed by Moulton Developments Ltd., and were being manufactured for BMC by Dunlop. Completing the suspension were normal telescopic dampers. Rack and pinion steering was used, and as the axle line was to the rear of the engine/gearbox assembly, and the steering rack to the rear of the axle line, the steering column was markedly more upright

A 1961 Morris Mini-Minor
De Luxe, pictured during
1967 and looking good for
considerable further use.

than on the conventional long-bonneted cars.

A subframe at the rear carried the independent rear suspension, in which the wheels were each located on the end of a trailing arm so arranged as to allow only truly vertical wheel movements. Rubber springing and telescopic dampers were to be seen again here.

Chosen to eliminate wheelarch intrusion into the passenger space, the 10 inch diameter roadwheels allowed only a 7 inch brake drum diameter; but, bearing in mind the relatively light kerb weight of little more than 12 cwt the 68 square inches of brake lining area seemed adequate enough, although high pedal pressures were indicated by the fact that the front brakes were only of the single leading shoe type.

The space-saving benefits of this, in parts, quite ingenius mechanical/running gear specification and general layout were to be seen in full when viewed as an integral part of the whole car. Measuring just 10 feet from bumper to bumper inclusive, being just 4 feet $7^1/2$ inches wide overall,

How luxurious can an Austin Seven get?

Austin Super Seven. 848 c.c.s. 4 forward gears. Price £405.0.0 plus £186.17.3 Purchase Tax and surcharge

You'll never know till you've seen the Super Seven

Just whether the impressive His 'n Hers headgear was available as an optional extra is not actually made clear in this 1961 advertisement introducing the new Super Seven Austin Mini.

and standing only 4 feet 5 inches high, the BMC Mini was nevertheless a genuine four-seater car with all the important internal dimensions closely matching, and in some cases even exceeding those of the externally much larger four-seaters which had hitherto made up the small-car sector. The two-door bodyshell was a simple monocoque structure, to which, as has already been mentioned, a pair of subframes carrying the mechanical elements were attached. Longitudinal ribs, beginning just aft of the front footwells and continuing to under the rear seat position, and a small central tunnel through which ran the exhaust pipe, were sufficient to provide adequate underbody stiffness.

Although in its frontal appearance there was a hint of Morris Oxford Series 2, styling for its own sake had been avoided, with just a sensible rounding-off at the corners of a shape determined wholly by packaging considerations. A large glass area giving good visibility was nevertheless not too large so as to look out of proportion with the rest of the car. Chrome plating was to be seen on the bumpers, door handles, headlamp surrounds, grille surround on the Morris-badged car, and complete grille on the Austin version which featured wavy horizontal bars as seen on some other Austins. Overriders were to be found on the De Luxe models, which also came with full diameter bright metal wheel covers rather than just the hubcaps of the standard car.

Hinged at its rear, the small bonnet top opened to reveal a tightly-packed compartment, in which the carburettor was somewhat inaccessible between the engine and scuttle, whereas in contrast the plugs were very easy to reach at the front. There was simply no room for the battery under here, and so that item was transferred to the rear where it resided in the offside of the luggage boot. A $5\frac{1}{2}$ gallon fuel tank occupied the entire nearside of this compartment, whilst the spare wheel was kept horizontally in a central recess in the floor. A rubber mat covered both wheel and battery, and in order to make the best use of the small luggage space a set of fitted suitcases was available as an optional extra.

Access to the passenger compartment was well up to the accepted two-door standards; the doors were wide, and both front seats could be tipped forward for easy entry to the rear. Seat cushions slightly shorter than average, and particularly the very thin squabs helped in providing adequate kneeroom, which in the rear remained at 8 inches when the front seats were at the rearmost of their 4 inches of adjustment. There was also further stowage space inside the car. A large parcel shelf was provided across the front, and another optional extra was a shaped container which could be stowed under the rear seat, whilst each door and rear side panels included a deep compartment of useful width. The provision of horizontally sliding windows in the doors had made the stowage space here possible by obviating the usual window-winding mechanism; simple cable "pulls" were used to release the door catches from inside the car. On the De Luxe models the rear side windows could also be opened, being hinged at their

The Mini lent itself well to the estate car theme, although looking somewhat austere as illustrated without the timber decoration available on more expensive versions.

AUSTIN

mini countryman

Fully equipped to de-luxe specification, it has all the motoring refinements such as fresh-air heater, windscreen washer, and ashtrays, so necessary for the pleasure and convenience of the modern family.
For conversion to goods-carrying duties, merely fold down the rear seat, and there in an instant is 36 cu. ft. (1·02 m.³) of goods space accessible through the double-opening rear doors. Floor to roof, the last cubic inch is usable, because there is a mirror fitted on each front wing, in addition to the tinted interior mirror, to provide satisfactory rearward vision for the driver. Sleek and stylish, the incredible Austin Mini Countryman becomes the businessman's best salesman—a brilliant tribute to his business, whatever it may be.

leading edge, whilst other De Luxe features were two-colour seats, carpeting rather than rubber mats, windscreen washers and, rather surprisingly, a heater unit. The latter however was only a cheap recirculatory type. Both standard and De Luxe models were without the usual facia board, with just a single circular speedometer protruding from the centre of the scuttle beneath the screen; included in this dial were the fuel gauge, and warning lights for ignition and low oil pressure. Also placed centrally were switches for the heater, wipers, ignition, and choke, situated in the deep lip of the parcel shelf and requiring a considerable stretch forward by the driver when needed.

Despite its tiny overall dimensions, the Mini was very definitely a "real" car in all respects, and with prices of just £497, or £537 for the far better-equipped De Luxe, it was greeted with considerable enthusiasm and immediately recognised as a major breakthrough in small car design.

Able to nudge 75 mph flat out, and reach 60 mph from rest in around 27 seconds on the one hand, whilst being capable of returning better than 50 mpg on the other, the Mini was well to the fore amongst small cars in these respects, whilst in terms of roadholding and stability it was setting new standards. On the debit side, the ride quality was poor, and not helped by the small seats which could prove uncomfortable over long distances. And there were teething troubles too. Minis spluttering to a halt with soaked ignition systems in wet weather were not uncommon, and neither were Minis with sodden carpets. Waterproof covers for the distributor and coil, which were mounted immediately behind the grille, were the cure for the former, but stopping water leaking into the footwells was much more difficult and only eventually overcome by redesigning the joint area where the floorpan met the body sides.

Whilst these problems had shown up straightaway, the variety of mechanical faults which also afflicted the Minis took a little longer in terms of both time and mileage to manifest, and as a result the model was to come in for many under-the-skin changes over quite a number of years which improved its reliability out of all recognition by comparison with some of the earliest examples. Despite some of its problems, not all of which were serious anyway, the Mini quickly began to attract a wide following, endearing itself to all manner of people offering as it did a certain combination of qualities which simply could not be purchased elsewhere.

Early in 1960 a Minivan with a useful 5 cwt capacity appeared, being simply the front end and doors of the saloon with an extended box-like van body to the rear, and on a wheelbase lengthened by 4 inches to exactly 7 feet. This spacious little vehicle was an ideal basis for an estate car, and these duly appeared in September 1960 as the Austin Seven Countryman and Morris Mini Traveller. The van proportions were retained, but with added-on timber framework, and full length glazing which included sliding windows. A slight disappointment were the twin van doors at the rear rather than a lift-up tailgate, as these doors resulted in a wide centre blind spot being encountered when using the rearview mirror. With all seats occupied, by virtue of 9³/₄ inches extra length the estate car offered greater luggage space than the saloon, whilst further goods-carrying capacity was obtained by tipping the rear seat cushion forward and dropping the squab flat in a manner similar to most estate cars.

The estate car was set a little higher on its suspension than were the saloons, but there was no change in the mechanical specification. With only a small increase in unladen weight the performance penalty was slight, and at £623 the model offered useful savings over the Austin A40 Countryman (£660) and Morris Minor 1000 Traveller at £669.

"Super" versions of the saloons were added to the range in September 1961, at £592, and for which the buyer received a much better trimmed and rather quieter Mini than the cheaper De Luxe and standard models which were continuing as before. Improved seating now featured foam-padded cushions, and their pleated design was now repeated on new vinyl door and rear side trims. Heavy sound-deadening underfelt beneath new carpets now covered the floor, with additional felt lining on the body panels and a sound-deadening application in the wheelarches. An oval instrument panel housed the Super's speedometer, which was now flanked by gauges for engine temperature and oil pressure. The cheap recirculating heater remained as standard, but a fresh air heater could now be specified at extra cost. More refined, these Super Minis had put on a little weight, and as the 848 cc engine was continuing unchanged there was just a slight performance decrease by comparison with the cheaper models, but a much higher-performance version was also now making its debut in the form of the Mini Cooper.

By virtue of the amount of tuning equipment for them which had quickly become available from outside sources, the Minis had already become a very popular choice for the enthusiast, and to racing car constructor John Cooper, himself a Mini owner, an off-the-peg go-faster Mini seemed assured of considerable success. Hence the Mini Cooper, powered by a long-stroked A-Series derivative of 997 cc. Curiously, the bore size was reduced by a mere half millimetre, to 64.2 mm, with this being in conjunction with a new crankshaft of much longer throw giving a stroke of 81.2 mm. With twin SU carburettors, larger inlet valves, double valve springs, and a compression ratio of 9.0:1, the Mini Cooper engine developed 55 bhp at 6000 rpm, and 54 lbs/ft torque at 3600 rpm. This was transmitted to the front wheels through a close-ratio gear set controlled by a new short remote control gearlever. The final drive ratio remained as on the lower-powered Minis, as did the tyre size although the latter were now a high-speed version of Dunlop's C41, being of nylon-cord construction. Disc brakes on the front wheels were another change which took into account the higher speed potential.

With almost exactly 85 mph available, and an ability to accelerate from rest to 60 mph in 18 seconds, the Mini Cooper possessed a performance previously only associated with much larger-engined saloons, and with a trim level broadly similar to the new Mini Super models it quickly proved to be an attractive proposition at £679.

Closely following the announcement of the Super and Cooper Minis, came badge-engineered Wolseley Hornet and Riley Elf derivatives, at £672 and £694, respectively, and with the emphasis here being on further luxury. The traditional Wolseley and Riley upright radiator grilles, hitherto seen only in front of elegantly-long bonnets, looked rather out of place on the snub-nosed Minis, but did serve to differentiate these from their lesser stablemates. A lengthened boot which, thanks to the body side panels being extended to form mildly-finned rear wings, avoided the added-on look, was another instant recognition feature. Capable of taking an extra 2 cubic feet or so of luggage, and increasing the car's overall length by 8 inches, this boot had a lift-up lid rather than the drop-down affair of the ordinary Minis, and was complete with a carpeted wooden floor panel. On the Wolseley, the oval instrument panel introduced on the Mini Super was to be seen, but was given a wood veneer finish, whilst on the Riley Elf there was a full facia board for the first time on a Mini, and including drop-down lids for glove compartments each side of the central instrument cluster. This facia was also veneered, with the two lids and central instrument panel being in a

The sheer convenience of the Mini in congested conditions lead to many buyers who could have afforded much larger cars. Aimed at such people were coachbuilders Harold Radford's luxury conversions which became available during 1963.

contrasting wood to that of the facia board. A chromed gearlever was unique to the Riley, and this model's combination of simulated leather and cloth upholstery gave it a rather more expensive air than the Wolseley which had plastic-covered seats. The heaviest of the Minis so far, these Wolseley and Riley versions required around 30 seconds to reach 60 mph from rest, but would still just manage an honest 70 mph maximum.

During early 1962 the "Seven" title was deleted from the Austin-badged cars which now became simply Austin Minis. In October that year the whole range benefited from the adoption of baulk-ring synchromesh; although still unfortunately only on the upper three ratios, this synchromesh transformed the Mini's gearbox which had so far earned a very poor reputation in this respect. The Super and De Luxe Austin/Morris cars were now amalgamated into a Super De Luxe, and an estate car without the wood framework was added to the range. A purchase tax reduction early in 1962 was followed by another tax reduction at the end of the year, and the Austin/Morris Minis went into 1963 unopposed at £447 (standard), £493 (Super De Luxe), and £531 and £551 for the all-steel or timber-decorated estate cars, respectively. For comparison, the Ford Anglia was £514, £538, and £574 in its standard,

De Luxe, and estate car versions.

A Mini Cooper was now £567, and the Wolseley Hornet/Riley Elf models were listed at £550 and £575. These last two models were now boasting leather upholstery, and were further improved early in 1963 when the standard recirculatory heater gave way to the fresh air type. Both the Hornet and Elf became Mk 2 models in March 1963 with the introduction of a 998 cc A-series engine specifically for these Wolseley and Riley cars. This unit had a bore measurement of 65.58 mm in conjunction with the 76.2 mm stroke of the original A-series power units of the Austin A30 and A35. The compression ratio was 8.3:1, and with its single SU carburettor the 998 cc engine developed 38 bhp at 5250 rpm. This enabled the Hornet/Elf duo to at least outperform the down-market Austin/Morris Minis by acceleratng from rest to 60 mph in 24 seconds and continuing to a maximum 77 mph.

The Mini Cooper eventually received a tuned version of the 998 cc unit when it lost the long-stroked 997 in January 1964. With the same 55 bhp as before, but now at the slightly lower 5800 rpm, and an increase in torque output to 57 lbs/ft but at only 3000 rpm these latest Mini Coopers were rather livelier than before, and possessed a 90 mph maximum now as the shorter-stroked unit proved willing to rev much harder in top gear than had the superseded long-stroked engine.

Since April 1963, running alongside the "ordinary" Mini Coopers had been the Mini Cooper S which was being produced in small numbers apparently as a homologation special suitable for international rallies, and with a unique 1071 cc A-series engine. In April 1964 came additional 970 S, and 1275 S Mini Coopers, so enabling B.M.C. to enter production cars in the up-to-1000cc, up-to-1100cc, and up-to-1300cc classes in the major rallies. In the event, the 1071 S and 970 S had been deleted by early 1965, leaving the 1275 S which in addition to being the basis of an outstanding competition car, was also enjoying considerable sales success.

Meanwhile, the ordinary Austin/Morris Minis were proving immensely popular, selling to people in all walks of life, including the rich and famous, and in so doing proving to be Britain's first "classless" motor car. What on the face of it had looked like serious opposition had appeared in 1963 in the form of the Hillman Imp, but in the event this had proved incapable of making a significant impact on Mini sales.

In September 1964 the Mini range, including, rather surprisingly, the Cooper and Cooper S, received the Hydrolastic interconnected suspension as first seen on the Morris 1100 two years earlier. With this set-up, which had needed quite considerable tailoring to incorporate into the much smaller Mini, these now had a rather softer ride but at the expense somewhat of the handling qualities which were not now quite so crisp as before. A big improvement now however, on the all-drum-braked Minis, was the adoption of two-leading-shoe front brakes. A diaphragm-spring clutch was also introduced at the same time, whilst needle-roller bearings replaced ball-races on the gearbox layshaft.

This change in the gearbox was typical of the continuous development that had been taking place since the Mini's release, and which had resulted in many more unseen changes being incorporated in the interests of improved mechanical reliability and longevity. In respect of the engine, for example, these had by now included a larger oil pump, improved crankshaft bearings, and changes to the timing gear.

Widening the Mini's appeal still further, in September 1965 came the announcement of automatic transmission as an optional extra, at £92, although production problems were in fact to delay its general availability for some time. This was the Automotive Products design, with torque

With the adoption of a larger engine during 1963, both the Riley and Wolseley variations became Mk 2 models.

BMC themselves were also offering luxury variants of the Mini theme in the shape of the Wolseley Hornet and Riley Elf.

converter and four forward speeds, and either fully automatic selection or manual over-riding control. A higher final-drive ratio came with this optional transmission, giving a restful 17.2 mph/1000 rpm on top gear. Thus equipped, the Mini was inevitably slow off the mark, and in fact required some 37 seconds in which to reach 60 mph from rest; it would however still manage a genuine 70 mph, and with its higher gearing there was less adverse effect on its fuel economy than is usually the case with automatic versus manual transmission.

Curiously, the automatic option was not being offered on the Wolseley Hornet and Riley Elf derivatives, and these models continued unchanged until being considerably upgraded in other respects in October 1966 with the introduction of wind-down windows, push-button door handles, face level air vents, and the Mini Cooper-type remote-control gearchange. Elf/Hornet Mk 3 designations accompanied these improvements.

Meanwhile, the ever popular Austin/Morris Mini models continued virtually unchanged throughout 1966 and into the following year until, in October 1967, the Austin, Morris, and Cooper Minis went into Mk 2 form as a result of several small but worthwhile changes, plus the availability at last of the single carburettor 998 cc engine on the ordinary Austin/Morris-badged versions. At this stage, eight years after its introduction, the Mini was still unique and regarded as something of a phenomenon. Today, incredibly still in production, fully-sorted and as such arguably the most reliable new-car buy around, its transverse-engined front-wheel-drive layout has also been so widely copied as to be the accepted norm for small economical saloons.

Datapanel: Austin/Morris Mini, Mini Cooper

	Mini	Mini Cooper (998 cc)
Engine	4 cyl, ohv	4 cyl, ohv
Capacity	848 cc	997 cc (998 cc)
Bore	62.92 mm	62.43 mm (64.58 mm)
Stroke	68.26 mm	81.28 mm (76.2 mm)
Compression ratio	8.3:1	9.0:1
Max BHP	34 nett @ 5500 rpm	55 nett @ 6000 rpm (55 nett @ 5800 rpm)
Max torque	44 lbs/ft @ 2900 rpm	54 lbs/ft @ 3600 rpm (57 lbs/ft @ 3000 rpm)
Gearing	14.9 mph/1000 rpm	14.9 mph/1000 rpm
Tyres	5.20 x 10	5.20 x 10
Kerb weight	12 cwt	12$^1/_2$ cwt
Overall length	10 ft	10 ft 0$^1/_2$ in (with overriders)
Overall width	4 ft 7$^1/_2$ in	4 ft 7$^1/_2$ in
Wheelbase	6 ft 8 in	6 ft 8 in
Performance		
	"The Autocar" 28th August 1959	"The Motor" R/T No. 35/61 (997 cc)
Max speed		
Top gear	72.7 mph (mean) 74.5 mph (best)	85.2 mph (mean) –
3rd gear	61 mph	63 mph
2nd gear	40 mph	46 mph
1st gear	24 mph	28 mph
Acceleration		
0–30 mph	6.2 seconds	4.8 seconds
0–50 mph	16.9 seconds	11.8 seconds
0–60 mph	26.5 seconds	17.2 seconds
0–70 mph	–	26.3 seconds
0–80 mph	–	47.3 seconds
	Top gear/3rd gear	Top gear/3rd gear
20–40 mph	12.6/8.6 seconds	11.8/7.6 seconds
30–50 mph	14.3/10.0 seconds	12.7/7.9 seconds
40–60 mph	19.9/15.6 seconds	13.3/9.4 seconds
50–70 mph	–/–	16.5/– seconds
60–80 mph	–/–	30.6/– seconds
Fuel consumption	40.1 mpg (1422 miles)	34.6 mpg (1064 miles)

Some six months before the Mini made its appearance, Alec Issigonis's design team began scheming out a somewhat larger car of exactly the same layout, in which the objective this time was to provide quite generous four-seater accommodation, but still within relatively compact overall dimensions.

Although a scaling up of the Mini theme, this was not to be an actual scale-up of the Mini car itself, instead being a completely new car designed from scratch around the new dimensions chosen for this particular package. An overall length and width of 12 feet $2^1/4$ inches, and 5 feet $0^1/4$ inch, and a wheelbase of 7 feet $9^1/2$ inches, when allied to the transverse engine/transmission concept were quite sufficient to allow a measure of styling to be introduced to the bodywork this time whilst still providing impressive interior space.

Of monocoque construction, the bodyshell was in either two- or four-door form, although only the four-door model was to be available in Britain, and was braced longitudinally by the box-section sills and a central tunnel. A transverse box-section member ran inside the floorpan beneath the front seats, whilst another similar member formed the base of the rear bulkhead. The four doors gave good access to a passenger compartment in which the principle dimensions, apart perhaps from floor to roof, were such as found previously only in externally much larger cars, and were therefore outstanding for a car of this modest size. Individual front seats were one-piece mouldings in a plastic/fibre composition, and like the more conventional rear bench seat were covered in I.C.I.'s Vynide, with that company's Vynair being used for the foam-backed roof lining which was

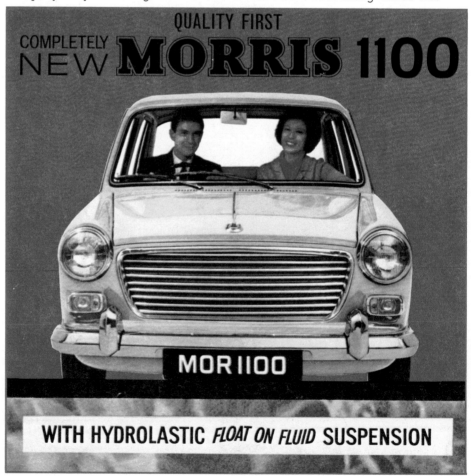

QUALITY FIRST
COMPLETELY NEW **MORRIS 1100**

WITH HYDROLASTIC *FLOAT ON FLUID* SUSPENSION

A measure of styling for its own sake was incorporated in the 1100 series . . .

bonded to the steel shell. Yet another grade of vinyl was used for the door trims, whilst use of vacuum-formed plastic mouldings was made elsewhere in the interior. Unlike the Mini, this car was not intended to be sold at rock-bottom prices, so although basic and De Luxe versions were to be on offer both featured fully trimmed doors with wind-up windows, and therefore even the basic model was without the rather stark "economy" look of the Mini. Additional equipment of the De Luxe included a passenger's sunvisor, front door pockets, and padded upper rear quarter panels on which passengers could rest their heads. The heater was optional in each case, and a rather plain steering wheel was used for both models, but the speedometer directly in front of the driver was a nicely stylised affair and neatly shrouded. Apparently making a first appearance on a British car was a facia-mounted warning light which would indicate a blocked engine oil filter. Cubby holes, without lids, on either side of the speedometer were supplemented by a full width parcels shelf running beneath, and as on the Mini there was further stowage space under the rear seats.

A gently sloping tail concealed a larger luggage boot than the outside appearance suggested, and in detail the arrangements here differed from the Mini. The fuel tank, now of $8^1/2$ gallons capacity, resided horizontally between the rear wheels and was shaped along its rearmost side to partially embrace the spare wheel which also lay flat in the extreme rear. A false floor covered these items, and this conveniently shaped compartment was accessed via a self-supporting lift up lid.

A slightly longer bonnet than was strictly necessary to house the transverse engine was used, although from an aesthetic point of view was still too short to properly balance the car's lines. Overall however, with this longer nose and rear side bodywork extended to form mildly-finned rear wings, and the provision of larger roadwheels, this model looked altogether more "grown up" than the Mini. Nevertheless, the overall visual impression was still of a functional rather than stylish car.

The slight increase in frontal length in combination with the greater width

... and particularly at the rear where a suggestion of fins could be seen. This brochure illustration points out the compact overall dimensions of this nevertheless quite roomy car.

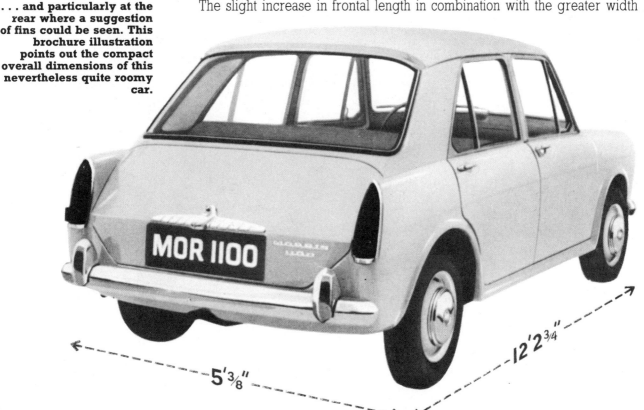

5'3⅜"

12'2¾"

Comfortable four-seat accommodation was indeed provided, and in altogether more well-appointed surroundings than in the smaller Mini models.

Pictured as recently as 1984, BOE 199C displays the wavy grille design which accompanied the Austin badge on the 1100 range.

of this car did result in improved underbonnet accessibility, whilst also allowing the battery to reside here now rather than in the boot. Looking similar externally, and working in exactly the same manner as already described for the Mini earlier in this book, the power pack differed internally in that the engine was of greater capacity, whilst the final drive ratio was lower in order to compensate for the bigger diameter roadwheels. A capacity of 1098 cc was the largest up to that time from the A-series unit, and was achieved by increasing both bore and stroke measurements which were now 64.57 mm x 83.72 mm. The longer-throw crankshaft necessary at this capacity was a substantially strengthened affair similar to that of the Mini Cooper, featuring thicker webs and a torsional vibration damper, and ran in lead-indium main and big-end bearings. The cylinder head used the larger inlet valves of the Mini Cooper, and gave a compression ratio of 8.5:1. With just a single SU carburettor there was 48 bhp at 5100 rpm, with the peak of the torque curve occurring at 2500 rpm where 60 lbs/ft was developed.

Baulk ring synchromesh, which the other small BMC models would inherit, was a worthwhile improvement in the otherwise virtually unchanged transmission, apart from its final drive ratio now amended to give the same 14.9 mph/1000 rpm overall gearing as on the Mini despite the larger wheels.

This whole unit was again mounted on a subframe which it shared with the front suspension units, and rack and pinion steering gear just as on the Minis. At the rear the layout was also again as on the smaller car, with each wheel at the end of a trailing arm, and the whole arrangements forming another sub-assembly to be attached to the underside of the bodyshell.

Although utilising the rubber cone springing, a big difference now was that in place of the usual separate hydraulic damper to be found at each corner of the car, the front and rear spring units were linked hydraulically; this being the "Hydrolastic" system which was a further development by Moulton. The coupling of the suspension units was simply fore-and-aft, so each side still acted independently. This system worked on the principle that when one wheel encountered a bump and was therefore raised, it pushed the fluid in the connecting pipework towards the other suspension unit which then exerted a downward pressure on its wheel so forcing the body at that end upwards. Up-and-down movements of the car over rough and uneven surfaces were therefore rather more vertical than with a conventionally-suspended car over which the same road surface irregularities would be traversed in a mildly see-saw manner and, broadly speaking, all the more so the shorter the wheelbase length. By reducing this see-saw, or pitching tendency, the Hydrolastic suspension would therefore go some way towards overcoming an inherent drawback of the short wheelbase inevitable when building a small car. An anti-roll bar, fitted at the rear, was another departure from the Mini, as was the provision of front disc brakes for this larger car. Unique at the time, the 12 inch diameter road wheels were shod with Dunlop C41 tyres of the size 5.50 x 12 being

A different instrument too for the Austin-badged cars.

the AUSTIN 1100 countryman

manufactured solely for the new BMC model.

Announced in mid-August 1962, badged solely as a Morris, and with "1100" sufficing as a model name, this second version of Alec Issigonis's novel theme was priced at £675 and £695 in its four-door standard and De Luxe editions, to which £13/15/0d extra had to be paid if the heater was required.

In respect of passenger accommodation the Morris 1100 was unbeatable at these prices, and on this consideration alone its sales success was assured. There were also other qualities hard to find at the price, including a very good ride by small car standards, exceptional roadholding perhaps bettered only by the Mini at that time, and which was accompanied by remarkably roll-free cornering too. Unfortunately, however, the Hydrolastic suspension was not self-levelling in respect of load carrying, and coped far less-well under heavy load conditions than did the conventional rear longitudinal leaf spring suspension systems. With the boot well-laden at a time when the 1100's rear seat was occupied by the three persons for which there was indeed room, the car assumed a tail down attitude so marked as to appear faintly comical in daylight whilst being infuriating to oncoming road users after dark by seriously upsetting the dipped headlamp beams.

A maximum speed of 78 mph, and a figure of around 23 seconds for the 0 to 60 mph dash were near to what was expected of the larger, $1\frac{1}{2}$ litre family cars of the day, and were accompanied by good response from medium speeds in top gear which, in conjunction with the car's excellent stability under most conditions, could result in very quick point to point times. The rather low overall gearing which helped produce the good acceleration did not however result in poor fuel consumption as might have been expected, with the figures in the 30 to 40 mpg bracket which most owners would achieve being perfectly reasonable for this 16 cwt car.

Within two months of the new car's release there appeared a rather more sporting version; this being the MG 1100 which was recognisable as such by its squarish MG-style grille. With twin SU carburettors, improved valve porting, a freer-flow exhaust system and a raise in compression ratio to 8.9:1, the 1098 cc engine in the MG developed 55 bhp at 5500 rpm. As the gearing remained unchanged, this modest increase in power output was sufficient to achieve useful if not spectacular improvements in acceleration, and a near 10 mph gain in maximum speed at which the engine was however turning over at a very audible 5800 rpm. This MG was, therefore, much more of a sprinter than an easy high speed cruiser, but it offered much the same fuel economy from its higher-efficiency engine as did the lower output unit of the Morris. Better quality seat coverings, an imitation-wood facia (later changed to real wood veneer) and a strip type speedometer were changes to be seen inside the MG 1100. The heater was also standard equipment on this better appointed car for which an extra £117 over the price of the Morris was being asked.

Both models benefited from the late 1962 purchase tax reduction and went into 1963 at new low levels of £592 and £611 for the standard and De Luxe Morris models, and £713 for the MG. Other cars available at similar prices to the Morris 1100 were Ford's Cortina four-door standard and De Luxe at £591 and £615, the Hillman Minx De Luxe and Vauxhall Victor standard each at £616, and BMC's own Austin A40 De Luxe at £599. Unique amongst these however in several respects, the 1100 series quickly set about capturing a large share of the market to become a best-seller in Britain quite early in its production life.

A near identical twin joined the Morris 1100 in September 1963 when an Austin 1100 appeared. Looking just the same externally apart from its Austin-style grille, this model differed internally where restyled seat coverings and door trims could be seen along with a new facia panel. The latter was now without the cubby holes, and featured an elongated speedometer similar to that of the MG. Mechanically identical to the Morris 1100, the Austin was also selling at exactly the same prices.

An appreciably more upmarket version was announced soon after the Austin, and was displayed at the 1963 Earls Court Motor Show although not actually going into production until early in 1964. This was the Vanden Plas Princess 1100. These cars were to be completed at the Vanden Plas coachworks, in Kingsbury, from part-finished cars supplied from BMC's

The frontal treatment was as on the saloons, with this example being the Morris 1100 Traveller.

Longbridge works. At Kingsbury they were fitted out with deep pile carpeting, real leather seating of which those in front had fully reclining squabs, and an exclusive polished walnut facia. The latter included a lockable glove box on the passenger side, and a retractable central ashtray above which was an electric clock. Two traditional-looking circular instrument housings faced the driver, and just to the right of these was an inset panel containing the switchgear. Walnut was also used for the door cappings and on the drop-down picnic tables situated in the backs of the front seat squabs.

The Princess-style grille, as already seen on much larger BMC products, blended in very well to the 1100's front end, and was flanked by a pair of auxiliary driving lamps. Special hubcaps, wheeltrim rings, and a neat coachline running the length of the car were other subtle embellishments which set the Princess 1100 part from the lesser models in the range. Powering this luxury 1100 was the 55 bhp version of the 1098 cc unit as already seen in the MG model, and which in the rather heavy (17^1/$_2$ cwt) Princess produced a performance somewhere between that of the Austin/Morris and the MG versions. At a rather hefty £895, the Princess was

Emphasizing the smooth riding qualities of the Hydrolastic suspension, this advertisement depicts the badge-engineered Wolseley 1100, with the two-tone division suggesting a slightly longer car than is actually the case.

If you're tired of all the thumping, bumping, rattling, rocking and rolling whenever road surfaces are less than perfect, it's time you had a luxurious Hydrolastic® Wolseley 1100

BACKED BY BMC SERVICE–Express, Expert, Everywhere.
BUY WISELY–BUY WOLSELEY 1100
£754.7.1 (including £131.7.1 p.t.)
Duotone model £769.9.2 (including £133.19.2 p.t.)

THE **BRITISH** MOTOR CORPORATION LTD.

W249

quite an expensive car for its size and performance, but nevertheless proved to be a fully justifiable addition to the big-selling 1100 series of cars.

The next, and final stage in the badge-engineering of the 1100 range came in September 1965, when a Wolseley 1100 and a Riley Kestrel appeared. These both used the 55 bhp engine of the MG variant, and were identified by the appropriate upright Wolseley and Riley grilles and which, unlike on the MG, were flanked in these two instances by low-set horizontal grilles

Datapanel: Austin/Morris 1100 & derivatives

	Austin/Morris	MG/Riley /Wolseley/Princess
Engine	4 cyl, ohv	4 cyl, ohv
Capacity	1098 cc	1098 cc
Bore	64.57 mm	64.57 mm
Stroke	83.72 mm	83.72 mm
Compression ratio	8.5:1	8.9:1
Max BHP	48 nett @ 5100 rpm	55 nett @ 5500 rpm
Max torque	60 lbs/ft @ 2500 rpm	61 lbs/ft @ 2750 rpm
Gearing	14.9 mph/1000 rpm	14.9 mph/1000 rpm
Tyres	5.50 x 12	5.50 x 12
Kerb weight	16 cwt	$16^1/2$ cwt ($17^1/2$ cwt Princess)
Overall length	12 ft $2^1/4$ in	12 ft $2^1/4$ in
Overall width	5 ft $0^1/4$ in	5 ft $0^1/4$ in
Wheelbase	7ft $9^1/2$ in	7 ft $9^1/2$ in
Performance		
	"Autocar" 17th August 1962	"The Motor" R/T No. 7/63 (MG 1100)
Max speed		
Top gear	77.7 mph (mean) 78.5 mph (best)	87.3 mph (mean) 89.8 mph (best)
3rd gear	64 mph	70 mph
2nd gear	41 mph	49 mph
1st gear	25 mph	28 mph
Acceleration		
0–30 mph	6.2 seconds	5.9 seconds
0–50 mph	15.2 seconds	14.7 seconds
0–60 mph	22.2 seconds	20.2 seconds
0–70 mph	36.9 seconds	30.2 seconds
0–80 mph	–	48.2 seconds
	Top gear/3rd gear	Top gear/3rd gear
20–40 mph	11.7/7.7 seconds	12.9/8.2 seconds
30–50 mph	12.4/9.3 seconds	13.5/9.2 seconds
40–60 mph	15.3/12.3 seconds	15.4/10.1 seconds
50–70 mph	22.8/– seconds	20.1/14.9 seconds
60–80 mph	–/–	29.9/– seconds
Fuel consumption	32.7 mpg (1916 miles)	30.0 mpg (814 miles)

which extended to include the sidelamps. The facia layout and elongated instruments on the Wolseley were exactly as on the MG 1100, whereas the Riley Kestrel had a more traditional layout comprising three circular housings; the outer ones being a speedometer and rev counter, whilst that in between housed the fuel, oil pressure, and temperature gauges. The prices for the sporting variations of the 1100 theme were now £742 (MG), £754 (Wolseley), and £781 for the Riley.

The Austin/Morris 1100 saloons were listed at £614 and £644 at this time (late 1965) in their standard and De Luxe guises, and for which the heater unit was now included in the De Luxe cars. For an extra £92 Austin/Morris 1100 buyers could now specify the AP automatic transmission, but this was not made available on any of the sporting derivatives.

Also only available in Austin/Morris versions were estate cars which made their first appearance as late as March 1966. These had the usual "Countryman" and "Traveller" name tags for the Austin and Morris-badged models, respectively, and in many ways made the best use yet of the spacious 1100 series bodyshell. Only two passenger doors were fitted, and aft of these were large side windows which could be opened by sliding fore-and-aft. The full width rear tailgate opened from the compartment floor level, and these estate cars had seating which could be arranged in a variety of ways including if necessary a double-bed arrangement. At £699 the Traveller and Countryman were sound value alongside such as the Triumph Herald estate car at exactly the same price. It was a pity, though, that no attempt had been made to counter the tail-down attitude when laden which has already been mentioned in connection with the 1100 saloons. This situation was at its worst on the estate car, which had the accommodation for very heavy loads, but with which headlamp adjustment was necessary for safe travel after dark.

By the time the estate cars appeared this larger version of the Mini theme had already been in production for 3¹/₂ years, throughout which no serious changes in the specification had proved necessary. During its development period the 1100 had benefited considerably from experience being gained with early production Minis, and so had avoided some of the teething troubles of the smaller car. As the mileages built up, however, the constant velocity joints in the front wheel drive arrangements proved to be a weak point, and so new gaiters better able to retain the grease in the joints whilst guarding against the ingress of dirt were introduced to give these components a longer life. Other troubles with the 1100s seemed to be more random, and not infrequently indicative of a rather poor build quality which for some reason seemed to be evident on these models by comparison with other BMC cars of the period.

A susceptibility to serious corrosion at an early age was also becoming apparent, with the undersides generally, and the rear subframe in particular, suffering to an extent which could lead to the too-early demise of one of these cars if not caught quickly. The model's good points, however, ensured its continued success as one of Britain's top selling lines, and after going into a slightly revised Mk 2 configuration in 1967 the range carried on into the 1970s before its eventual production demise.

The Morris Minor
remained outwardly as
before when the 1098 cc
engine was first adopted.
The increase in power
was perhaps most
valuable in the
load-carrying estate car.

**MORRIS MINOR 1000
(1100cc)**

Running alongside the modern range of products from its own BMC stable,
the venerable Morris Minor which had first appeared back in 1948
eventually reached the one million production figure in December 1960. By
this time it had undergone several changes, including a completely new
engine and transmission line in 1953, and a major rework of this in 1956
which had helped keep it reasonably competitive in respect of speed and
acceleration amongst its more modern contempories.

The engine was of course the BMC A-series, now in 948 cc form and
being shared in this same capacity with the Farina Austin A40 from the same
stable. With this unit and its associated four-speed gearbox the Minor would
exceed 70 mph and reach 60 mph from rest in around 33 seconds, and
generally return better than 35 mpg even under the hardest of driving.
Backing this up were good road manners provided by the torsion bar
independent front suspension and rack-and-pinion steering gear, each of
which had remained virtually unaltered since the Minor's debut twelve years
before. At the rear, although softened somewhat in 1958 by reducing the
number of leaves from 7 to 5, the two semi-elliptic springs locating the rear
axle offered only an average ride quality by 1960 small-car standards.

Whilst having received a much larger window area in 1956, and other
subtle panelwork changes over the years, the Minor's sturdily-built
monocoque body retained its original well-rounded shape which in the early
1960s was completely out of fashion. Rather short on luggage space, and not
particularly well-endowed with passenger room either in relation to its
overall size, the Minor was also trimmed in a rather plain manner, and with
its brake and clutch pedals still coming up through the floorboards the
interior scene added to the old-fashioned impression which the car now
gave. These facts, coupled with the small-car developments taking place
within BMC, were such that it would have been no surprise if the Minor had
been deleted at the end of 1960 following the production of the one-millionth
example.

However, the Minor still had a strong following amongst people who

really did appreciate a well-proven design, and to whom styling trends, and indeed the latest technological developments came well down their list of priorities, and so for buyers such as these the Minor remained in production. In fact, whilst avoiding the complexities of BMC's front-wheel-drive developments, the Minor was nevertheless able to benefit from some of this work as it did of course include further development of the A-series power unit. Rationalization therefore benefited the Minor considerably late in 1962 when it received the much-strengthened 1098 cc A-series engine which had been evolved for the new front-wheel-drive Morris 1100. Baulk-ring synchromesh rather than the earlier constant-load type, and the raised 2nd gear of the new Morris 1100 were also now incorporated into the Minor's specification. A change in rear axle ratio from 4.55:1 to 4.22:1, and slightly larger, 5.20 x 14 tyres (5.00 x 14 previously) combined to give a sensible 16.2 mph/1000 rpm which imparted a rather more effortless feel to these latest Minors whilst ensuring that low fuel consumption remained as an attractive feature of the car.

With 48 bhp now to propel its 15 cwt-plus bulk the Minor was well up to the mark now in terms of performance for this class of car, and with more than 75 mph available an increase in front brake drum diameter to 8 inches giving a total lining area of 79 square inches (7 inch diameter all-round and 64 sq.in.previously) kept the stopping power in line with the increased urge If used to the full, the new found acceleration could induce quite considerable axle tramp on all but the best road surfaces now; but this was unlikely to worry the great majority of Morris Minor buyers, who of course were choosing this car because of its relative lack of sophistication with which came a virtual guarantee of very-long-term dependability.

Bearing in mind the well-proven nature of the design as a whole, prices ranging from £515 (standard two door-saloon) to £574 for the four-door De Luxe saloon early in 1963 represented quite good if not outstanding value for money alongside the Minor's much more modern contemporaries. The Ford Anglia was listed at £514 and £538 (De Luxe), whilst the cheapest Triumph Herald was at £552, and BMC's own alternative in the conventional small-car class, the Farina Austin A40, was starting at £556. A Minor Tourer (convertible) was quite a bargain at just £515 alongside the only other

Post October 1963 models featured restyled side/direction indicator lamp units. 5544 MT is in fact a 1966 car which today has only covered 21,000 miles from new.

Another beautifully-preserved Minor, this time the ever-popular Tourer.

Datapanel: Morris Minor 1000

Engine	4 cyl, ohv
Capacity	1098 cc
Bore	64.6 mm
Stroke	83.7 mm
Compression ratio	8.5:1
Max BHP	48 nett @ 5100 rpm
Max torque	60 lbs/ft @ 2500 rpm
Gearing	16.2 mph/1000 rpm
Tyres	5.20 x 14
Kerb weight	15 $^1/_2$ cwt (4 door)
Overall length	12 ft 4 in
Overall width	5 ft 1 in
Wheelbase	7 ft 2 in
Performance	
	"The Motor"
	R/T No. 2/63
	(4 door)
Max speed	
Top gear	76.0 mph (mean)
	80.0 mph (best)
3rd gear	67 mph
2nd gear	44 mph
1st gear	26 mph
Acceleration	
0-30 mph	6.4 seconds
0-50 mph	17.2 seconds
0-60 mph	26.0 seconds
0-70 mph	44.6 seconds
	Top gear/3rd gear
20-40 mph	14.0 / 8.7 seconds
30-50 mph	13.4 / 9.9 seconds
40-60 mph	17.2 / 13.1 seconds
50-70 mph	33.7 / -- seconds
Fuel consumption	36 mpg (1614 miles)

soft-top contender at this end of the market which was the Triumph Herald convertible at £642, and completing the range was the Minor Traveller (estate car) which was also looking good enough at £581 between the Ford Anglia estate car (£574) and the corresponding Triumph Herald this time at £664.

So, the Minor continued, selling quite well and still coming in for slight revisions from time to time. A fresh-air heater (still an optional extra) replaced the old recirculatory type in April 1963, and in October that year an overlapping windscreen wiper arrangment at last replaced the old "blind centre spot" set up which had curiously remained for so long as a relic of the Minor's much earlier split-windscreen days. For 1965 came safety type crushable sunvisors, a plastic-framed interior mirror, and a slightly changed facia in which the passenger side cubby hole lid made a reappearance after being deleted some years previously. A combined ignition/starter switch was introduced; but the dished, and rather elegant sprung three-spoked steering wheel unfortunately now gave way to a cheaper looking and flatter two-spoked affair, and which somehow served to detract from the "traditional" appearance of the car's interior appointments. A self-supporting boot lid arrangement in place of the hand-positioned stay which had sufficed for so long was perhaps the most welcome improvement.

A falling-off in sales during the latter part of the 1960s, and the company merger which resulted in the formation of British Leyland signalled that the end was in sight for the Minor. The first to go was the Tourer, in 1969, leaving the saloons and the Traveller to soldier on until just into the next decade.

Simple, but tasteful trim continued to be a feature of the late-model Minors, although some of the elegance was lost when the earlier spring steering wheel was replaced with the type shown here. The strap type doorpulls were a neat touch. The (relatively) cramped conditions serve to give the impression of a rather more cosy interior than on the Minor's ultra-modern front-wheel-drive contempories from BMC.

2

FORD

**ANGLIA,
ANGLIA SUPER**

In 1956, following the introduction of the Mk 2 versions of their Consul/Zephyr range, Ford of Britain turned its attentions to an eventual replacement for the sidevalve-engined 100E Anglia and Prefect models which were now into their third year of production.

An expansion programme, begun at Dagenham two years earlier, meant that by the 1960s the company would have far greater productive capacity which would allow for a new range of medium-size cars to come between the small Anglia/Prefect type and the much larger Consul/Zephyr series. These new medium cars would obviate the need for a small four-door model, and so bearing this in mind the projected new Anglia 105E was to be designed exclusively around a two-door layout, rather than having to accommodate four-door variants as with all the preceding small Fords.

By this time already experienced in the design of monocoque structures, Dagenham now came up with a relatively lightweight but extremely sturdy bodyshell for the new car, and with a pleasing shape arrived at partly as a result of wind-tunnel testing, but also taking into account the comfort and convenience of rear seat passengers to a far greater extent than usual in small passenger saloons. With crossmembers situated at each end of the passenger area, and longitudinal chassis-like box-section members continuing over the rear wheelarch pressings to the rear, the underbody bracing was substantial. The rear wings formed part of the integral structure, with a further aid to rigidity at the rear being Dagenham's usual rather high back panel. This arrangement allowed a full-width luggage compartment, in which the spare wheel was stowed vertically immediately behind the rear seat. Located in a shallow well in the boot floor, the wheel was secured at the top by a strap, this being considered a useful improvement over the 100E model in which the spare wheel had resided horizontally on the boot floor. The repositioning of the fuel tank, now beneath the boot floor rather than inside the left-hand rear wing as previously, also aided the provision of a more convenient and roomier luggage compartment. A ratchet type self-supporting strut held the wide boot lid in the open position.

Designed to accommodate Ford's then still patented MacPherson strut independent front suspension system, the front end structure consisted of robust inner front wings with longitudinal stiffeners along their lower edge, and turret-like upper suspension mounting points. From these the suspension loads were transmitted rearwards into the substantial scuttle/bulkhead

62

the world's most exciting light car!

This is the day of the all-new Anglia—the car that's really different, *really exciting*. Exciting to look at: exciting to drive! TAKE A LOOK! *At its radical new styling*—low cut to gain every ounce of power. *At its rear window*— raked back for extra rear headroom and greater visibility all round. *At its engine*—997 c.c. O.H.V., over-square—first ever to be fitted to a British light car. *At the speedometer*—up to 75 m.p.h., up to 50 m.p.g.! *At the four-speed gearbox*—with stubby floor lever and slick, quick sports car changes. This is the full-four-seater car that's got more good looks, gives more comfort, more room, more driving pleasure than any other in its class. The car that's built above all for the sheer joy of motoring. That's why we call it the world's most exciting light car!

the all-new ANGLIA

BE FIRST ON THE ROAD WITH FORD

This launch-date advertisement for the 105E Anglia captures the excitement which always seemed to accompany a new car launch in those days. The De Luxe model is shown here in both views, and complete with the optional dual-tone paint.

structure and, via the windscreen pillers, into the roof. Opening at its rear edge, a full-width bonnet top curved downwards to the front where it was hinged to the low front panel, with this curvature having been decided largely as a result of aerodynamic testing.

Unique with its reverse-slope rear window, the passenger compartment gave comfortable room for four persons within very compact external dimensions. Giving excellent rear headroom for this class of car, the reverse-slope rear window design also allowed the rear seat to be placed well back with the result that comfortable rear kneeroom was still provided when the driver's seat was adjusted to its rearmost position. No adjustment was provided for the front passenger seat, but both front seats tipped forward for rear compartment access which was also aided considerably by the $39\frac{1}{2}$ inch width of the doors.

PVC trim was in single tone on the standard model, but in dual tones on the De Luxe on which the seating could also be specified in rayon-weave or leather; a moulded rubber floorcovering and a vinyl rooflining was common to both models. Window winding mechanism in both doors, each of which also included a positive locking hinged front quarter window, were a standard feature, whilst forward hinged opening rear side windows appeared on the De Luxe car only. A large, stylized speedometer faced the driver, and was matched in shape by the glove box facing the front passenger seat; this was lidded on the De Luxe car only, the speedometer housing of which also included an engine temperature gauge in addition to

The estate car featured a different rear wing line from that of the saloon, and came with an offside wing mirror as standard equipment, and the larger tyres which would also have benefited the saloon considerably from the appearance viewpoint alone.

the fuel gauge which was the only supplementary instrument on the standard model.

A stalk control appeared on either side of the deeply-dished steering wheel, that on the left being solely for headlamp dipping, whilst the other was Dagenham's first application of the multi-purpose stalk in that it controlled both the horn and direction indicators. Another "first" on a Dagenham car now were the electrically operated windscreen wipers replacing the vacuum type which, with their annoying tendency to cease working at wide throttle openings, had angered so many small-Ford owners in the past.

Externally, differing degrees of bright metal trim identified the standard or De Luxe model Anglias. Chrome plated bumpers, hubcaps and door handles were to be seen in both cases, but whilst the standard model had just a narrow front grille with a painted finish, the De Luxe car boasted a full width affair in bright metal. A front screen surround, a full length side strip, and tail lamp housings also in a chrome finish completed the De Luxe

Anglia's embellishments. Two tone paintwork in which the roof panel and rear quarter pillars received the second colour could also be specified when ordering a De Luxe car, on which twelve single tone, and four extra-cost dual schemes were available. Only eight single colours could be had on the standard model.

Under the bonnet, at last replacing the so-familiar 1172 cc sidevalve engine came a completely new 997 cc overhead valve unit of considerably oversquare dimensions with bore and stroke measurements of 80.9 mm x 48.4 mm. This was the first engine of Ford's now legendary "Kent" series of power units. Despite its unusually large bores for so small a capacity engine, a feature of the new cylinder block was water jacketing encircling each separate cylinder and thus ensuring the desirable even cooling properties so often sacrificed by the use of siamezed bores in compact engines. Cast in Dagenham's own foundry, the extremely short-throw crankshaft was hollow throughout its length, and featured unusually large diameter (1.93 inches) big-end journals by 1 litre engine standards. With such generous dimensions in conjunction with so short a throw there was considerable bearing journal overlap adding to the rigidity of this lightweight crankshaft to such an extent that extremely low bearing loads were achieved without the need to include counterbalance weights.

The cast iron cylinder head featured bathtub shaped combustion chambers, with these being fully machined and therefore each of closely matching volume providing an accurate 8.9:1 compression ratio. Separate inlet ports were another feature of this cylinder head, which carried its pushrod operated overhead valves vertically and in line. A single Solex carburettor was used, with which the new engine produced 39 bhp (nett) at 5000 rpm, with the peak of the torque curve occurring at 2700 rpm at which 52.6 lbs/ft was developed.

With more than a million Anglias produced many have survived, and depicted here during 1988 the near perfectly preserved 1263 NE displays the model's characteristic lines.

Accompanying this modern engine was an equally new gearbox, notable in that it was providing four forward speeds for the first time on a Ford car. Intelligently spaced ratios, of which third gear offered a vastly improved overtaking performance by comparison with earlier small Fords, were a nice feature of this gearbox as was also an excellent floor mounted gearchange. The lack of synchromesh on first gear however was a slight disappointment. An open propeller shaft took the drive to a new hypoid-bevel rear axle assembly with a ratio of 4.125:1. This gave overall gearing which, at 16 mph/1000 rpm, was rather high by the small-car standards of the day, and suggested that the new Anglia would cruise easily on the forthcoming Motorway network.

Whereas this powertrain owed nothing to preceding small-Ford design, the running gear did follow closely that of the superseded 100E Anglia. The usual Ford MacPherson strut independent front suspension, located by track control arms and a transverse anti-roll bar was of course to be seen, as was also the Ford/Burman steering gear but with the steering box now being of the extremely light to operate recirculating ball type rather than the worm and peg variety of the 100E range. At the rear were longitudinally mounted leaf springs of considerably greater length than on the preceding models, and offering improved roadholding in addition to softer riding qualities. The beam rear axle was located $1\frac{1}{2}$ inches forward of the leaf spring centre, with the spring's forward mounting point being lower than those at their rear. This arrangement, along with the provision of additional bump stops ahead of the axle, was chosen to limit any spring wind-up tendencies. Completing the rear suspension came Armstrong lever-arm type shock absorbers.

Whilst promising to be a faster car than the 100E, the new model was however very slightly lighter in weight, and the previous car's Girling

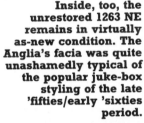

Inside, too, the unrestored 1263 NE remains in virtually as-new condition. The Anglia's facia was quite unashamedly typical of the popular juke-box styling of the late 'fifties/early 'sixties period.

hydraulic braking system with an 8 inch diameter drum measurement and 76.8 square inches of lining area were considered adequate enough once more. Of the same width again, but with closer spacing of the four-stud fixing, came 13 inch roadwheels and 5.20 x 13 tyres.

The Anglia made its appearance in September 1959, at just £589 and £610 for the standard and De Luxe models, but to which £14 had to be added in both cases if the heater/demister unit was required. At these prices the 105E was undercutting BMC's popular A40 Farina by around £40, and as that car was some £50 lower than the new Triumph Herald aimed at the same market, it seemed certain that the Anglia would be an outstanding success. On the road, with a genuine 75 mph available, and an ability to reach 60 mph from rest in 27 seconds the Anglia was more than just competitive in terms of performance. Its fuel economy potential, too, was excellent, with

Datapanel: Ford Anglia, Anglia Super

	Anglia	Anglia Super
Engine	4 cyl, ohv	4 cyl, ohv
Capacity	997 cc	1198 cc
Bore	80.96 mm	80.96 mm
Stroke	48.41 mm	58.17 mm
Compression ratio	8.9:1	8.7:1
Max BHP	39 nett @ 5000 rpm	48.5 nett @ 4800 rpm
Max torque	52.6 lbs/ft @ 2700 rpm	63 lbs/ft @ 2700 rpm
Gearing	16 mph/1000 rpm	16 mph/1000 rpm
Tyres	5.20 x 13	5.20 x 13
Kerb weight	14$^{1}/_{2}$ cwt	15 cwt
Overall length	12 ft 10 in	12 ft 10 in
Overall width	4 ft 9 in	4 ft 9 in
Wheelbase	7 ft 6$^{1}/_{2}$ in	7 ft 6$^{1}/_{2}$ in
Performance		
	"The Motor"	"The Motor"
	R/T No. 25/59	R/T No. 48/62
Max speed		
Top gear	75.5 mph (mean)	81.8 mph (mean)
	76.9 mph (best)	84.2 mph (best)
3rd gear	70 mph	68 mph
2nd gear	37 mph	38 mph
1st gear	23 mph	22 mph
Acceleration		
0–30 mph	6.2 seconds	5.1 seconds
0–50 mph	16.7 seconds	13.8 seconds
0–60 mph	26.9 seconds	21.6 seconds
0–70 mph	40.0 seconds	34.9 seconds
	Top gear/3rd gear	Top gear/3rd gear
20–40 mph	14.5/9.0 seconds	12.3/7.7 seconds
30–50 mph	16.1/10.9 seconds	13.1/8.8 seconds
40–60 mph	21.6/17.9 seconds	14.6/12.3 seconds
50–70 mph	–/–	21.0/– seconds
Fuel consumption	39.3 mpg (1002 miles)	33 mpg (1619 miles)

better than 45 mpg available at a constant 50 mph. Good roadholding and handling qualities accompanied the Anglia's useful performance, and this coupled with the willingness and unburstable nature of the ultra short-stroked engine quickly endeared the model to many an enthusiastic driver motoring on a limited budget.

Whilst its small size, neat styling, and mostly delicate colour schemes gave the Anglia an almost dainty look, it was in fact a remarkably rugged product. This was demonstrated conclusively in the tough East African Safari Rally when, in both 1960 and 1961, the Anglias soundly defeated the well-known German opposition in the small-car categories to take 1st, 2nd, and 3rd in class on each occasion. These results were just some of the highlights in the Anglia's competition career which was to stretch for several years and include outright victory in the BRSCC Saloon Car Championship in 1966.

The saloons were joined by an estate car late in 1961, this featuring a completely restyled rear end in which the saloon's rear wing line and tail lamp treatment disappeared. A counterbalanced lift up tailgate was provided, giving access to a 35 cubic feet load space of 54 inch length when the rear passenger seat squab was folded flat. A painted wooden floor for the loading area sufficed for the standard model, with the rather better equipped De Luxe featuring a heavy-duty linoleum covering complete with alloy rubbing strips. Obviously intended to cope with some overloading, were seven-leaf rear springs in place of the saloon's four-leaf equipment. Larger tyres – 5.60 x 13 – were also fitted, but more than offsetting these in respect of their effect on the gearing was a 4.444:1 rear axle ratio which gave an overall 15.3 mph/1000 rpm. Weighing in at almost 1 cwt more in the unladen state than the saloon, the estate car was inevitably a little slower off the mark, but still proved capable of reaching an honest 70 mph. Anyone now ordering an Anglia saloon could specify the estate car's lower final drive ratio as a no-cost option, and with which the Anglia's flexibility was improved but at the expense somewhat of the model's acclaimed high speed cruising abilities.

Engine tuning specialists had been quick to realise the potentialities of the 105E engine, and by this time Anglia owners had a wide choice of tuning equipment from which to choose should they wish to increase the performance of their little Ford. Reworked cylinder heads, twin SU carburettor set-ups, different camshafts, and even superchargers were all available. Thus modified the Anglia could become a very potent car indeed, and in order to tame the performance when necessary disc brake conversion kits were soon being offered by outside sources.

Ford themselves offered a "Performance Plus" conversion kit during 1961, consisting of a larger Solex carburettor, new camshaft, stronger valve springs, and heavy-duty main bearing shells. Having little effect on maximum speed, but improving both acceleration and flexibility, this was good value at £13 when ordered on a new car, but was rather less so when ordered retrospectively for fitting by a Ford agent, when an £11/10s/0d fitting charge was imposed.

An interesting feature of the Performance Plus conversion was that it eliminated a flat spot in the carburation which had afflicted a not inconsiderable number of Anglias, and on which had proved difficult to eradicate. This problem was finally solved early in 1962 with the introduction of a new Solex carburettor, incorporating an accelerator pump in its design, into the production Anglia specification. For owners of earlier Anglias suffering from this flat spot phenomenon, but now outside the warranty period, the new carburettor was made available through Ford agents at cut price.

In October 1962, following closely upon the appearance of the new Cortina, the Anglia range was extended with the introduction of the Anglia Super. This came complete with the Cortina's 1198 cc version of the "80 bore" engine, all synchromesh four-speed gearbox, and braking system with 81.7 square inches of lining area. The result of this specification was an Anglia which could exceed 80 mph, reach 70 mph from a standstill in 35 seconds, and with a braking performance to match. Additionally, the Super came equipped with fitted carpets, a padded facia top, "metallic" finish PVC trim, rear compartment grab handles, cigarette lighter, windscreen washers, twin horns, and the heater unit. Distinctive two-tone paintwork with which additional chrome side strips outlined a contrasting colour flash, and wheeltrim rings easily identified the Anglia Super on the road.

The standard and De Luxe saloons and estate cars continued unchanged, and with the benefit of a purchase tax reduction earlier in the year, plus a Ford price cut also the range was continuing to offer excellent value now at £514, £538, and £598 for the standard, De Luxe, and Super saloons; the estate cars were now £575 and £593 in their standard and De Luxe configuration. Welcome news for any prospective Anglia purchaser just wanting performance rather than luxury was that a "1200" package comprising the 1198 cc engine, all synchromesh gearbox, and the larger brakes could be ordered on any of the cheaper Anglias for just £24 extra cost.

With no further changes over the next two years Ford were able to lower prices considerably early in 1964, at which time the standard, De Luxe, and Super saloons were reduced to £478, £510, and £575 respectively. Slight trim changes for 1965 included the adoption of colour-keyed interior trim and paintwork combinations, a new "breathing" PVC seat covering for the Super, and the availability at extra cost of cloth trim throughout the range. The Anglia now continued strongly for a further two years before production ceased in November 1967 to make way for the all-new Escort which was to appear early in 1968.

CONSUL CLASSIC 315

Under development concurrently with the new Anglia, the medium sized Ford needed to fill the gap in the range of Dagenham's products was scheduled for release in early 1960, some six months or so after the Anglia's announcement. However, an even greater demand than had been anticipated for the new Anglia left Ford without any spare production capacity throughout 1960, and it was not until May 1961 that the new mid-range car appeared.

With its full title Consul Classic 315, the new car was the first indication that the familiar Consul name would soon disappear from the company's top-of-the-range four-cylinder models to become associated instead with the new mid-range series. Indeed, in export markets the new car was to be advertised and badged simply as the Consul 315; but despite this, and the Consul prefix in its home market guise, the British public quickly abbreviated it to "Classic", thus avoiding any confusion with the big Mk 2 Consul still in production.

Whilst its reverse-slope rear window gave it an obvious family resemblance to the Anglia, the Classic's bodyshell was appreciably longer, wider, and very slightly lower than its small stablemate. These proportions, accompanied by outer panel work cleverly styled to accentuate the sleek appearance, resulted in a perhaps even more distinctive looking car than the Anglia. Indeed, such were the styling touches incorporated in the shell that little in the way of additional embellishments were necessary, and even on the De Luxe model the considerable bright metal content was nevertheless somehow quite discreet, although the chrome strips running along the body sills did seem superflous. At the front, in addition to providing the Classic driver with excellent night time illumination of the road ahead, four headlamps played a prominent part in the overall styling. These flanked a small horizontal opening in the low front panel, and in which "floated" five chromed stars; this simple "grille" was surrounded by a bright metal strip, with a plain chrome plated bumper bar completing the front end trim. The extremities of the rear bumper were styled into the car's outline, and on the De Luxe only there was a silver satin-finish panel running beneath the boot lid. Twelve single tone colour schemes were available on both models, with a further seven dual tone options on the De Luxe for no extra cost.

Structurally, the underbody bracing of this bodyshell followed Dagenham's established principles, which had resulted in the robust Zephyrs and Anglias being the only British cars to not only habitually finish the East African Safari Rally, but collect major awards regularly in this event too. Within an overall length of 14 feet 3 inches an enormous luggage boot was provided, with sufficient room aft of the rear wheelarch to stow the spare wheel upright inside the nearside rear wing. Additional bracing of this cavernous compartment could be seen in the form of broad welded-in struts running

Styling considerations played a considerable part in the development of the Consul Classic 315. This Ford archive photo captures the model's lines very well, and in such pleasant surroundings.

676 VTW

diagonally upwards from the wheelarch to the wing top. The counterbalanced boot lid opened from immediately behind the rear window thus giving an extremely large opening, although baggage still had to be lifted over the rear body panel. Residing beneath the boot, protected on each side by the chassis-type longerons, was a 9 gallon petrol tank. The fuel filling arrangements were as on Dagenham's larger cars, with the filler cap being neatly concealed behind the spring loaded hinged rear numberplate.

As on the Anglia, the bonnet top was hinged along its front edge, whilst ensuring a good fit now when closed were catches at both rear corners, with these being released from inside by a single control. Of considerable area, the bonnet top featured cross-bracing substantial enough to suppress any tendency towards flexing.

Inside a wheelbase of 8 feet 3 inches was a passenger compartment of comfortable four-seat dimensions, and with room for five persons if required. Two- and four-door versions were being offered, with wide doors on the former and tip-up front seats of which the passenger's remained in the upright position without the need for being held in place, and giving about as good an access to the rear as could be reasonably expected in a two door car. As with the Anglia, good rear seat headroom was provided by the reverse-slope rear window.

Viewed through the dished steering wheel were a recessed horizontal speedometer flanked by projecting gauges for fuel level and engine coolant temperature; a lockable glove box faced the passenger, and the facia top was heavily padded. A full width parcel shelf ran beneath the facia, with this also being complete with a safety front edge. Single tone PVC upholstery, a rubber floor covering, and the surprising lack of a passenger's sunvisor characterized the standard model. Both cars featured swivelling quarter windows in all doors in addition to the main wind-down windows. Variable speed electric windscreen wipers, complete with anti-lift double rubbers were also standard equipment. Exclusive to the De Luxe Classic were screen washers, twin horns operated by a full circle hornring, twin sunvisors, a carpeted floor, dual tone PVC on both seats and doors, padded door armrests incorporating the door handles, coat hooks, cigarette lighter, rear ashtray, headlamp flasher, and front door operated courtesy light. The

Head-on view taken from a brochure illustration seems to suggest that a glamorous night-life is yours for the taking when you own a Consul Classic.

heater and demisting unit however was still only available at extra cost.

It was not only the distinctive profile which the new car was sharing with the Anglia, for beneath the Classic's smooth bonnet top was to be found a larger capacity version of the Anglia's power unit. Utilising the same cylinder block, with its 81 mm bores, but with a longer throw crankshaft now giving a 65 mm stroke, resulted in a swept volume of 1340 cc. As that of the Anglia unit, this new crankshaft was a hollow casting, and again devoid of counterweights. Whereas the latter feature was of no consequence on the Anglia unit, it was soon to be seen as a mistake on the 1340 cc engine which failed to match the smoothness of the 1 litre unit. Apart from the crankshaft and correspondingly short connecting rods, the internals of the new engine were almost wholly as on the smaller edition. An increase in cylinder head thickness lowered the compression ratio slightly to 8.5:1, and a Zenith accelerator pump type carburettor rather than the Anglia's Solex instrument ensured the Classic would not be troubled by the flat spot which had afflicted some early Anglias. In this configuration the Ford "80 bore" engine produced 54 bhp nett at 4900 rpm, and with 74 lbs/ft torque being available at 2500 rpm the 1340 cc would be well able to cope with the Classic's 18$\frac{1}{2}$ cwt bulk.

The transmission also was as on the Anglia, with the hydraulic clutch being of the same 7$\frac{1}{4}$ inches diameter, the gearbox utilising the same indirect ratios and still without the benefit of synchromesh on first gear. The excellent floor mounted gearshift was standard equipment, but buyers of the De Luxe model could specify a steering column mounted arrangement without any increase in price.

As was to be expected, the front suspension consisted of the MacPherson strut coil spring and damper units, each located by a track control arm and transverse anti-roll bar. No surprise also was the Burman recirculating ball steering box mounted safely behind the front axle line as had been standard Ford practice for so many years; from here it controlled the direction of the front wheels through the usual three-piece track rod arrangement. The rigid rear axle was located by a pair of half-elliptic leaf springs, with the axle being situated 3 inches forward of the spring centre. Ahead of the axle was an additional bump stop, and to be seen once again completing the rear suspension were Armstrong lever-arm dampers.

Whilst its suspension arrangements, like the engine and transmission, had closely followed the Anglia pattern, in respect of braking the Classic was taking a major step forward amongst inexpensive cars. For some months past the big Mk 2 Consul had been the cheapest car available with disc brakes, but this honour was now being transferred to the new Classic which was to be equipped as standard with Girling 9$\frac{1}{2}$ inch diameter discs for the front wheels. Servo assistance however was not considered necessary now as the Classic was some 4 cwt lighter than the much larger Consul; but like that car, the Classic did feature 9 inch diameter by 1$\frac{3}{4}$ inch width rear drums. Completing the running gear now came four-stud fixing 13 inch roadwheels with 5.60 x 13 tyres.

Never intended to be a bargain-basement model, and not matching the outstanding value for money usually offered by the largest Fords, the Classic was nevertheless very competitive value amongst its obvious rivals upon its release in 1961. At prices of £744 (standard 2-door), £773 (2-door De Luxe/4-door standard), and £801 for the four-door De Luxe car, the Classic was faced with such as the Austin A55 Cambridge at £801 and £829 in its standard and De Luxe forms, and Vauxhall's F series Victor of which the top model was also £801. Despite a power unit smaller than either of these, the Ford's maximum speed of 78 mph was at least their equal, whilst its through

Just as distinctive at the rear, the Classic was always unmistakable.

Interior view of the two-door De Luxe, showing door handle built-in to doorpull/armrest, and opening rear side window. In addition to ensuring good headroom, the reverse-slope rear window had the practical advantage of remaining clear in rain or snow.

the gears accelerative powers enabling it to reach 60 and 70 mph in 22 and 36 seconds was rather better. Able to return better than 30 mpg fuel consumption figures at cruising speeds in the 60 to 65 mph bracket, the Classic was notably economical in its class.

Coming as it did within the Ford range, placed nicely between the Anglia and the Consul, the Classic was particularly welcome to those who wished to stay loyal to Ford but to whom the generous six-seater proportions of the Mk 2 Consul were inappropriate.

The Classic received justifiable praise for its handling qualities, and particularly so for riding characteristics which were very good for this class of car. Adverse comments regarding the relative lack of engine smoothness by average four-cylinder standards could however be heard at times, and were valid enough. But, that the car also earned a reputation as being one which required considerable use of the gearbox if brisk progress was to be maintained, did need some qualifications. This reputation came about of course because here was a 1.34 litre car of not inconsiderable weight and, more importantly, with a carrying capacity previously only associated with somewhat larger-engined cars. Nevertheless, if the well-spaced indirect ratios were used with some intelligence then the Classic's progress was at the very least as brisk as its most obvious rivals from the 1½ litre class at the time.

Few Classic owners would ever need a roof rack! The petrol filler is behind the pull-down numberplate, and the bright metal rear panel inserts indicate a De Luxe model.

The foregoing, however, became somewhat academic in so far as new Classic buyers were concerned when, in August 1962, the model went into the 1½ litre category itself. The originally planned maximum stretch in capacity from the 1 litre "80 bore" engine had been just under 1400 cc, but a full 1½ litres had become possible now as improved production facilities at Dagenham had allowed the introduction of an additional cylinder block of exactly the same bore and bore spacings, but very slightly taller. This block could therefore accommodate a longer stroke, and the 72.7 mm now chosen resulted in a capacity of 1498 cc. Of perhaps even more importance, this revised cylinder block was also designed to accommodate a five-main-bearing crankshaft, and with this feature, plus counterbalancing now, the latest crankshaft imparted a new standard of engine smoothness by inexpensive four-cylinder standards. A single Zenith carburettor was retained, and with a compression ratio of 8.3:1 the 1½ litre unit produced 59.5 nett bhp at 4600 rpm. Accompanying this was 81.5 lbs/ft of torque at 2300 rpm, and together these figures implied a useful performance increase. The overall gearing remained as before, but first gear was raised slightly, and given the benefit now of synchromesh engagement as well.

A purchase tax reduction in the 1962 budget had resulted in Classic prices ranging from £723 to £779 for the four-door De Luxe, and as no increase in price accompanied the new engine the Classic was looking very good indeed alongside such as the new Hillman Super Minx (£805), the FB Victor De luxe (£799), and the new Austin Cambridge A60 De Luxe at £833.

Undeniably excellent value now in its class, the Classic could have been expected to remain in production for some years ahead; but in fact, due to revised thinking within Ford about the medium-size car market, the Classic's future was strictly limited. The company's new Consul Cortina to be released in September 1962 would offer similar accommodation, but in an appreciably lighter, and less expensive to produce package. Although this

75

Even with little in the
form of chromium trim,
the standard model
Classic retains
considerable eye-appeal.

This late model four-door
De Luxe is well-endowed
with optional extras; such
as the radio, whitewall
tyres, and wing mirrors
styled to complement the
Classic's sleek look.

Based almost wholly on
the Classic saloons
beneath the shoulder line,
the Consul Capri Coupe
was a sporting derivative
considerably removed
from the family-car
category.

car was not being thought of as a direct Classic replacement, a rather more up-market car based on similar thinking to the Cortina was. This appeared in October 1963 as the Cortina-derived Consul Corsair saloon, at which time the Classic made history having just completed Ford of Britain's shortest production run.

Datapanel: Ford Consul Classic 315

	Classic 1340 cc	Classic 1498 cc
Engine	4 cyl, ohv	4 cyl, ohv
Capacity	1340 cc	1498 cc
Bore	80.96 mm	80.96 mm
Stroke	65.07 mm	72.75 mm
Compression ratio	8.5:1	8.3:1
Max BHP	54 nett @ 4900 rpm	59.5 nett @ 4600 rpm
Max torque	74 lbs/ft @ 2500 rpm	81.5 lbs/ft @ 2300 rpm
Gearing	16.4 mph/1000 rpm	16.4 mph/1000 rpm
Tyres	5.60 x 13	5.60 x 13
Kerb weight	$18^{1}/2$ cwt	$18^{3}/4$ cwt
	$18^{3}/4$ cwt (4 door)	19 cwt (4 door)
Overall length	14 ft 3 in	14 ft 3 in
Overall width	5 ft 5 in	5 ft 5 in
Wheelbase	8 ft 3 in	8 ft 3 in
Performance		
	"The Autocar"	"The Motor"
	23rd June 1961	R/T No. 33/62
	(4-door De Luxe)	(4-door De Luxe)
Max speed		
Top gear	78.5 mph (mean)	80.7 mph (mean)
	79.0 mph (best)	85.7 mph (best)
3rd gear	70 mph	73 mph
2nd gear	42 mph	45 mph
1st gear	24 mph	30 mph
Acceleration		
0–30 mph	5.7 seconds	5.3 seconds
0–50 mph	14.1 seconds	13.3 seconds
0–60 mph	21.8 seconds	20.1 seconds
0–70 mph	35.4 seconds	31.4 seconds
	Top gear/3rd gear	Top gear/3rd gear
20–40 mph	12.2/8.0 seconds	9.8/6.7 seconds
30–50 mph	12.9/9.6 seconds	11.1/7.9 seconds
40–60 mph	15.6/12.9 seconds	13.5/12.0 seconds
50–70 mph	21.6/– seconds	17.4/– seconds
Fuel consumption	28.8 mpg (1185 miles)	25.8 mpg (1932 miles)

**ZEPHYR 4, ZEPHYR 6,
ZODIAC**

That their planned medium-range models would inevitably take some sales from the four-cylinder version of Ford's large-car series was not only acknowledged by the company but actively encouraged by transferring the much-respected Consul name to the new middle order cars. Therefore, when the new Mk 3 models appeared in April 1962 the four-cylinder car had acquired the name Zephyr which had previously been exclusive to the six-cylinder cars. Also linking the new Zephyr 4 in more closely now with the new Zephyr 6 was an identical wheelbase and front end panelwork (except the grille), whereas both previous Marks of Consul had featured a shorter engine compartment, appropriate to the four-cylinder engine, and a correspondingly shorter wheelbase.

Of similar layout to before, and on similar structural principles, the Mk 3 bodyshell was nevertheless completely new, and in fact possessed even greater torsional rigidity than that of the Mk 2. With large longitudinal box section members from its extremities terminating where they met transverse stiffeners running under the front and rear seat positions, and with these transverse members continuing outwards to link with the box section body sills, the underbody bracing was of a similar pattern to the preceding cars.

The Zephyr 4, one of the largest four-cylinder-engined cars on the market, offering full six-seat accommodation and appropriate luggage space. 6807 SC is a 1963 example, but seen in these two lovely poses as recently as 1988.

6807 SC again, showing the rear fins which were such excellent rear width/length indicators when reversing in confined conditions.

A change from the Mk 2 now, which had featured a single central jacking point each side, was to be seen in the additional outriggers linking the main longitudinal members to the sill extremities each including a socket for the jack.

On the same 8 ft 11 inch wheelbase as the Mk 2 six-cylinder cars, this latest bodyshell was very slightly longer than before, with the increase to be seen in greater rear overhang. This resulted in an extremely large and conveniently shaped luggage compartment, although Dagenham's adherence to great structural rigidity again included the inconvenience of a high back panel over which luggage had to be lifted. The spare wheel now changed sides, being situated within (almost) the nearside rear wing. Occupying a similar position to previously, but now being sunk into the boot and bolted into position rather than being strapped beneath the boot floor as before, was a 12 gallon fuel tank with its upper surface forming the boot floor centre. In this position it was once again situated between the chassis-like members, on which themselves the sturdy rear bumper mountings were attached. As this design was not of the crumple-zone type, the petrol tank therefore continued to enjoy the excellent protection from accident damage which had always been a good feature of the big Fords, and indeed of many other cars of the 1950s and '60s period.

At the front, the inner wings were of a different design to previously, having now to accommodate front suspension struts which were angled considerably inwards in order to achieve a lower bonnet line. Reckoned to be stronger than the inner wings of the Mk 2 (but unfortunately proving to be more corrosion-prone after some years service), these were not tied into the scuttle with the additional diagonal bracing which had characterized the underbonnet scene on the Mk 1 and Mk 2 cars. The new scuttle/bulkhead

79

A lower-set grille identified the Zephyr 4s produced from October 1963 onwards, and can be seen clearly here on this 1965 car. The overriders, wheeltrims, wing mirrors, and radio are all optional extras which someone has fitted to DWF 501C pictured here when still only six years old, and in near to new condition.

structure included blown glass fibre noise insulation which markedly reduced the mechanical noise entering the passenger compartment. The large bonnet top was counterbalanced, with the spring loaded mechanism on each side now being situated on the flat top section of the inner wing, rather than on the bulkhead as on the outgoing car.

Within the same 5 feet 9 inches overall width as before, by virtue of their curved doors with curved windows, the Mk 3 models were now offering even greater hip and shoulder room than the generously dimensioned Mk 2. Fore and aft, however, the situation was less satisfactory, for whilst the three persons easily accommodated on the front bench seat were well catered for, those in the rear had rather less kneeroom than was usual in large cars of the day.

As in past Ford big-car practice, the rear seat was mounted considerably ahead of the axle line in the interests of both riding comfort and lack of wheelarch intrusion. On the Mk 3 however, as the front windscreen was of appreciably greater rake than on the outgoing model, and the roof line lower, the front seat was placed further back. Maintaining correct relationship with the front seat were centre door pillars also slightly more rearwards than before, thus lessening the door gap by some $2^1/2$ inches and so also making rear seat entry and exit somewhat less easy than it should have been on such relatively large cars. Ironically, this situation was more noticeable on the Zodiac which, as the luxury model of the range, featured rather larger seats than the Zephyrs.

These points did not of course alter the full six-seater capacity, where internal width is the critical factor, and of which the Mk 3 was very well endowed. In all other aspects the interiors were setting high standards, with a trim level which eliminated the then usual painted metal surfaces to be seen in car interiors. Two levels of trim and equipment were to be seen on the Zephyr, with the four-cylinder car retaining links with the Mk 2 Consul in respect of its moulded rubber floor covering, bright metal facia inserts, and central horn button. On the Zephyr 6 were fully fitted carpets, a wood grain finish for the facia inserts, and a full circle hornring. The new Zephyr facia design bore a similarity to the later Mk 2s, with an elongated speedometer flanked by gauges for fuel level and engine temperature. These were directly in front of the driver, with a glove locker and parcel shelf situated on the passenger side; the facia top was well padded, and the twin sunvisors were of the crushable safety type. Two-speed electric wipers were standard, but the screenwashers, heater, and cigarette lighter were all extra-cost equipment.

Both cars were equipped with armrest/doorpulls on all doors, with the door handles being neatly incorporated into these, and either single or dual tone trim colours could be had to choice without extra charge. The standard trim material was once again PVC, with Saranweave cloth seat trim as a no-cost option, or real leather for which extra was charged. Pull-down centre armrests were provided as standard on the Zephyr 6 only.

The Zodiac featured a rather more plushy interior, with its deeper seats being upholstered in the new, and exceptionally soft "Cirrus" PVC material, with either Bedford cord or English crushed hide available at extra cost. Deeper facia padding extended downwards to a lower band of simulated walnut, along which were situated the various control knobs. A drop-down glove locker was at this level on the passenger side, blending in to the walnut panel when closed. A ribbon type rectangular speedometer, and circular gauges for engine temperature and fuel tank level were set into a simulated walnut panel above the steering column. The heater, screenwashers, cigarette lighter, and central armrests were all standard equipment on the Zodiac, as was also an electric clock, vanity mirrors, a trip milometer, and map pockets in the front door trims.

Externally, a most important identification feature was that whereas the Zephyrs were of four-light construction and with broad metal rear quarter pillars, the Zodiac was of six-light design with triangulated rear quarters consisting of an opening window. This Zodiac treatment resulted in a differently raked, and larger rear screen. Four $5\frac{3}{4}$ inch headlamps rather

A rather more stylish grille accompanied the six-cylinder engine, and so provided instant recognition. The handsome lines of the Zephyr 6 are well portrayed in this view from the Ford archives.

81

than the two 7 inch types of the Zephyrs, deeper bumpers complete with overriders, wheeltrims, and horizontal bright metal strips along the lower back panel were other features exclusive to the Zodiac. Each of the Zephyrs had their own individual grille design, and on the Zephyr 6 only a bright metal grille strip was to be seen along the lower edge of the boot lid, thus differentiating the two Zephyrs when viewed from the rear. All three models featured rustless bright metal front and rear screen surrounds, with this also being applied to the side window frames on the Zephyr 6 and Zodiac.

The power units for the new Mk 3s were uprated versions of Dagenham's long-established oversquare, overhead valve four- and six-cylinder engines which had first appeared late in 1950 in the original Consul and Zephyr cars. The "four" had always been simply two-thirds of the "six", thus maintaining many common internals between the two such as piston/conrod assemblies, bearing shells, and individual valvegear components such as the pushrods, rockers, valves and valve springs etc.

General features of this in-line Ford engine were a very robust deep-skirt cast iron cylinder block, with full water jacketing encircling each individual cylinder, and three- (4 cyl.) or four-main-bearing crankshafts, each of which were fully counterbalanced and featuring generous main and big-end bearing journal overlap. As greater power outputs were now being sought, stronger connecting rod bolts, and copper-lead rather than white metal

Interior decor, 'sixties style. A page from the Zephyr 6 brochure reveals an interior scene in which styling has played a considerable part. Broad pull-down centre armrests were provided for when the maximum passenger-carrying capacity was not required.

big-end bearing shells were being introduced to ensure similar longevity to that of the Mk 2 units.

With the same bore and stroke measurements of 82.55 mm x 79.5 mm as on the Mk 2 models being retained, giving 1703 cc and 2553 cc for the four- and six-cylinder units, the greater power outputs for the Mk 3 were obtained by mildly reworked cylinder heads and improved carburation. An increase in compression ratio from 7.8:1 to 8.3:1 was in conjunction with larger valves and smoother porting. Single carburettors, again of Zenith manufacture, were still considered adequate, and thus equipped the Zephyr power outputs were 68 bhp at 4800 rpm and 98 bhp at 4750 rpm for the four- and six-cylinder cars (59 & 85 bhp previously). The corresponding peak torque figures of 93 lbs/ft at 3000 rpm and 134 lbs/ft at 2000 rpm were virtually as before, except that that for the four-cylinder engine was higher up the revolution range.

Despite what some owners claimed, standard Mk 2 Zephyrs and Zodiacs were not 100 mph cars, and indeed neither would the Mk 3 Zephyr 6 prove to be either. However, it was desirable by this time to offer a genuine 100 mph top-of-the-range car, and so to ensure that it would just exceed the magic three figures the new Zodiac featured a different Zenith carburettor and a dual exhaust system. These modifications were claimed to be worth 5.5 bhp each, and thus raised the Zodiac's output by a further 11 bhp to a healthy 109 bhp nett at 4800 rpm.

The previous versions of this six-cylinder engine had powered earlier Zephyrs to numerous rally awards, including outright victory in the Monte Carlo, East African Safari, and RAC Rallies, as well as an outright win in the BRSCC Touring Car Championship in 1959 – there were few, if any, better proven units than this one, and it was good to see it embarking upon a third lease of life in the new Mk 3s.

Mated to these engines now came new four-speed gearboxes complete with synchromesh throughout, thus breaking away completely from the traditional Ford three-speeder with its unsynchronised first gear. There were two sets of indirect ratios, with those for the Zephyr 4 being lower than those on the six-cylinder models; both sets had ratios well matched to their respective engines, and the opportunity had been taken to include relatively high third gears giving a wide range for overtaking purposes. The gearchange was mounted on the steering column, and its operation came surprisingly close to matching the standards of accuracy achieved by the simpler three-speeder of the past. Axle ratios of 3.9:1 and 3.545:1 for the four- and six-cylinder models respectively, gave sensibly high gearing of 18.5 mph/1000 rpm and 20.3 mph/1000 rpm on top gear.

Borg Warner overdrive, or that company's Model 35 automatic gearbox were transmission options at extra cost on all three cars. With the overdrive the standard axle ratios were retained, as was the case on the six-cylinder models also with the automatic gearbox. When the latter option was specified on the Zephyr 4 however, this car also received the 3.545:1 axle of the "sixes" with which it proved to be rather overgeared. This fact, coupled with the power losses apparent with torque-converter transmission, was to result in the Zephyr 4 automatic being only a very leisurely performer.

The sharper inclination inwards of the MacPherson strut independent front suspension units has already been mentioned, and another slight change to the front end running gear was the adoption of a variable ratio worm in the recirculating ball steering box. This had approximately the same gearing as before (18.1:1) around the straight-ahead position, but with lower gearing towards the extremes of lock maintaining exceptionally light control during parking manoeuvres. In the interests of softer riding, only five leaves each

Throughout its production run the Mk 3 Zephyr 6 enjoyed stardom in the television police series "Z Cars", and was a popular model with many police forces in real life too. Policeman Roy Owen poses with his Zephyr patrol car, circa 1966, at a time when on regular patrol of the Cheshire section of the M6 motorway. Comparison with the illustration below of an unladen estate car shows just how much weight in emergency equipment these Zephyr patrol cars carried.

(six previously) now made up the longitudinal semi-elliptics at the rear. These were interleaved throughout their length with butyl rubber, whilst also there was thick rubber insulation where they were clamped to the rear axle, and the usual rubber shackle bushes were larger than normal. Armstrong lever-arm shock absorbers again completed the arrangements here.

A Girling hydraulic servo-assisted front disc/rear drum braking system was of similar dimensions to previously on the Zephyr 4, which retained the rear drum 9 inch diameter by $1^3/4$ inch width. This system, with its $9^3/4$ inch diameter front discs, was far more than just adequate for the six-cylinder cars also. Nevertheless, on the Zephyr 6 and Zodiac $2^1/4$ inch width rear drums were now fitted, with this change being introduced primarily to lengthen the rear shoe lining life to mileages the equal of those achieved by the front disc pads.

6.40 x 13 cross-ply tyres, and $4^1/2$ inch five-stud rims were used throughout, but with the Zodiac's tyres being of the nylon cord type suitable for sustained speeds beyond 100 mph.

In all, the Mk 3s represented a considerable development over the preceding models, and as a result were introduced at basic prices greater than before. However, with their introduction around the time of the April 1962 budget, in which a purchase tax reduction was announced, the Mk 3s appeared at tax-paid prices of £846, £929, and £1070 which were only £50 or so more than the outgoing Mk 2s.

Useful performance increases had been achieved throughout the range, with the new Zephyr 4's ability to reach 60 mph in 19 seconds whilst on its way to a maximum speed of 85 mph or so being a substantial improvement over the Mk 2 Consul. The new Zephyr 6 would now run into the middle 90s, with these speeds being some 5 or 6 mph better than the Mk 2 Zephyr/Zodiac could achieve, although in its acceleration in the lower and medium speed ranges this Zephyr was not a significant improvement over the lively Mk 2s. The new Zodiac, however, very definitely was, with its ability to reach 60, 70, and 80 mph from rest in 13, 18, and 24 seconds being excellent in 1962; as was intended, the Zodiac's maximum speed proved to be just over 100 mph. Touring fuel consumption figures in the 27 to 30 mpg range for the Zephyr 4, and only 2 to 3 mpg below these with the "sixes" were perfectly satisfactory for this size of car.

Criticism was levelled at the cars in respect of the limited rear seat kneeroom already mentioned, and when the Mk 3s made their first Earls Court Motor Show appearance in October 1962 they featured a revised seating layout. This had been achieved by widening the rear track by $1^1/2$ inches which, with corresponding alterations to the wheelarches and rear floor pan allowed the rear seat to be moved back by approximately 2 inches. This was a very worthwhile modification, which served to largely remove the only legitimate criticism of the Mk 3 range.

At the same time, the Zephyr 4's interior was brought nearer to the Zephyr 6 standard with the inclusion of the imitation wood finish for the facia and the elegant hornring, whilst the range as a whole was extended by the introduction of estate car variants. These were once again being produced as conversions by E.D. Abbott, of Farnham, in Surrey, who had produced earlier Consul/Zephyr estates. Much sleeker than the Mk 2 estate cars, these latest models had the benefit also of a lift-up tailgate which seemed a big improvement over the previous side-hinged door. Moulded in fibreglass, the tailgate included a full width window, and with its slim rear pillars the estate car retained the excellent all-round vision of the Zodiac whilst improving upon that of the Zephyr saloons with their broad rear quarter panels. Ford

Capable of swallowing vast, and heavy loads, the big Mk 3 Fords nevertheless retained a lot of style in estate car configuration.

Zodiac front and rear corner close-ups from contemporary sales literature. Much of the Zodiac's brightwork was in polished rustless alloys.

had reduced their basic prices now, with the three saloons representing excellent value now at just £773, £837, and £971 for the luxury Zodiac, with the corresponding estate cars being £1051, £1115, and £1249.

As no one else was building such a large, but inexpensive four-cylinder car the Zephyr 4 was unopposed at its price, but the two six-cylinder Fords were faced with stiff competition now from the new Vauxhall Velox and Cresta PB Series which at £822 and £919 were also well to the fore in the value-for-money stakes.

A detail change for 1964 were the restyled overriders with rubber inserts. By now, less than £1000 was required to buy this large, lavishly-appointed, and so smooth-running 100 mph six-cylinder saloon.

Restyled seat and door trims were to be seen on the Zephyrs at the 1963 motor show in October, at which time the Zodiac received a pair of built-in reversing lamps, and rubber inserts in restyled overriders. Individual front seats had been an option for some time previously, and these were complimented now by the availability of an optional floor-mounted gearchange. This item could also be specified if a bench seat was being retained. A redesigned clutch pedal introduced early in 1964 dispensed with the assist spring, and improved clutch operation, whilst on the engine valve stem oil seals of a superior quality rubber were also introduced about this time; these cured a tendency for high mileage engines to burn some oil due to it leaking past brittle valve stem seals. In June 1964 a new offside front

Sporting its own distinctive grille and headlamp treatment, and glass rear quarter panels, the luxury Zodiac completed the Mk 3 range. A 1962 example, 664 ELW is pictured here during 1988, and is a well-known and popular exhibit at many northern Classic Car events.

coil spring was introduced, being 3/4 inch longer than its opposite number and said to correct the uneven tyre wear due to driver-only occupation – exactly what the situation was now with the front seat fully occupied was apparently not disclosed!

Moving somewhat out of the inexpensive six-cylinder saloon market, at a price of £1303, early in 1965 came the Zodiac Executive. This was in effect a

Datapanel: Ford Zephyr 4, Zephyr 6, Zodiac Mk 3

	Zephyr 4	Zephyr 6 (Zodiac)
Engine	4 cyl, ohv	6 cyl, ohv
Capacity	1703 cc	2553 cc
Bore	82.55 mm	82.55 mm
Stroke	79.5 mm	79.5 mm
Compression ratio	8.3:1	8.3:1
Max BHP	68 nett @ 4800 rpm	98 nett @ 4750 rpm (109 nett @ 4800 rpm)
Max torque	93 lbs/ft @ 3000 rpm	134 lbs/ft @ 2000 rpm (137 lbs/ft @ 2400 rpm)
Gearing	18.5 mph/1000 rpm	20.3 mph/1000 rpm
Tyres	6.40 x 13	6.40 x 13
Kerb weight	23 cwt	24^1/$_2$ cwt (25 cwt)
Overall length	15 ft	15 ft (15 ft 2 in)
Overall width	5 ft 9 in	5 ft 9 in
Wheelbase	8 ft 11 in	8 ft 11 in
Performance	"Autocar" 27th April 1962	"Autocar" 10th April 1964 (Zephyr 6 Automatic)
Max speed		
Top gear	84.0 mph (mean) 85.5 mph (best)	93.3 mph (mean) 95.0 mph (best)
3rd gear	67 mph	–
2nd gear	42 mph	64 mph
1st gear	22 mph	40 mph
Acceleration		
0–30 mph	5.3 seconds	5.6 seconds
0–50 mph	13.4 seconds	11.7 seconds
0–60 mph	19.6 seconds	16.5 seconds
0–70 mph	32.1 seconds	25.5 seconds
0–80 mph	–	35.9 seconds
	Top gear/3rd gear	Top gear/intermediate
20–40 mph	13.2/7.7 seconds	6.8/6.4 seconds
30–50 mph	14.8/8.4 seconds	9.5/7.4 seconds
40–60 mph	17.2/10.8 seconds	11.3/8.6 seconds
50–70 mph	21.2/– seconds	15.1/– seconds
60–80 mph	–/–	19.2/– seconds
Fuel consumption	23.8 mpg (711 miles)	19.1 mpg (1291 miles)

Zodiac automatic with all the other extras such as hide upholstery, reclining seats, seat belts, radio, wing mirrors, spot and fog lamps etc. About this time, the Zodiac's dual exhaust manifold was altered to feed the gases into a new large-bore single system, with which the Zodiac now lost its rather distinctive "rasp" when accelerating hard.

Production continued until the end of 1965 when the Mk 3s were phased out to make way for the completely new large Fords scheduled for release in April 1966, and in which nothing of the Mk 1, 2, and 3 series would remain.

CONSUL CORTINA, CONSUL CORTINA SUPER, CONSUL CORTINA GT

With the BMC's revolutionary new Mini undercutting Dagenham's equally new Anglia by a useful margin in the price lists, Ford were to lose the position they had held at the bottom of the market since the early 1930s as manufacturers of the lowest-priced car available in Britain. Having reasoned correctly that at its price BMC were losing money on every Mini sold, whereas the Anglia was making healthy profits, Ford accepted this new situation for them of being undercut at the economy end of the scale. As a result of this however, they were now very keen indeed to reinforce their generally accepted position of always offering something quite simply representing the best sheer value for money available anywhere.

A cheapened version of the forthcoming Consul Classic would not be appropriate as rock-bottom prices in the medium-size sector had not been in mind when this car was conceived. What was needed now was another medium-sized model planned from the outset to offer all the accommodation, convenience, and the performance of the typical roomy $1^1/2$ litre-engined models, but at prices previously only associated with much smaller cars.

The basis of the new car, which would be badged as the Consul Cortina, was a new monocoque structure in which considerable attention had been given to reducing weight; styling excesses, which themselves can increase weight, were carefully avoided. Welded on front wings aided the rigidity of this lightweight structure, which also retained in its make-up Ford's established underbody bracing layout. The result was a car which, when equipped with the optional front bench seat, could justifiably claim to be of occasional six-seater proportions, and with luggage space to match, yet would weigh in ready for the road at just 16 cwt in its two-door form.

Within a wheelbase of 8 feet 2 inches (1 inch less than the Classic) great care had been taken in planning the interior layout, with the rear seats being sufficiently ahead of the axle line to avoid wheelarch intrusion and give reasonably good headroom within the conventionally-sloping rear window design. Knee-room in the rear compartment was between 8 and 13 inches depending upon front seat adjustment, and bearing in mind the large luggage boot provided, the interior planning represented a considerable achievement in a car of 14 feet 2 inches length. Standard and De Luxe models were to be offered, both of which included a moulded rubber floor covering and PVC trim; the latter however was in dual tones and of a more elaborate pattern on the De Luxe car. Swivelling front quarter windows, and main-window winding mechanism in all doors were standard equipment; the rear side windows of the two-door cars were hinged at their front edge on the De Luxe, whilst being non-opening on the standard model.

Viewed through the simple two-spoked steering wheel was a raised binnacle housing an elongated speedometer, on one side of which was the only other instrument, in the shape of a fuel gauge; warning lights sufficed for other information. A usefully sized full width parcels shelf ran below the facia on both models, but the twin padded sunvisors, padded facia top, and

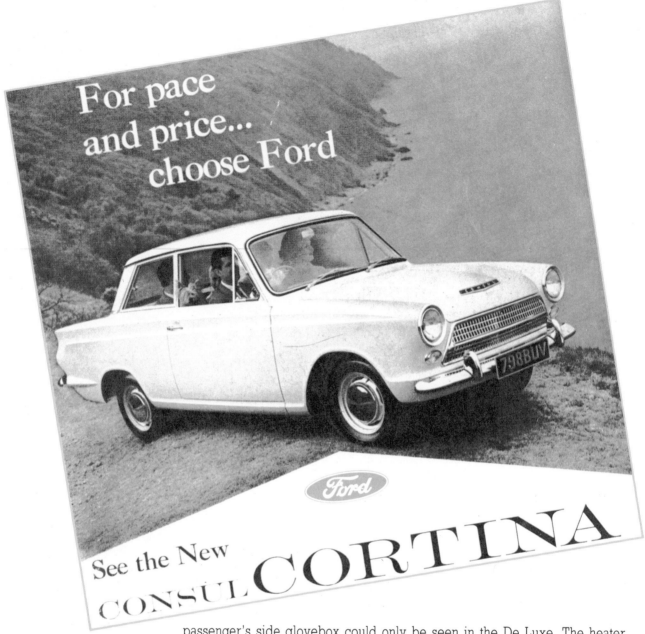

For pace
and price...
choose Ford

See the New CONSUL CORTINA

Only the two-door models were available at first. The De Luxe car illustrated here is equipped with the optional overriders.

passenger's side glovebox could only be seen in the De Luxe. The heater and windscreen washers were extra-cost options in both cases.

A counterbalanced boot lid opened to reveal a near perfectly shaped, and very large luggage compartment in which the spare wheel was housed vertically in the nearside wing, and an 8 gallon fuel tank was sunk into the floor and bolted in position as on the latest Zephyrs. At the front, a cheapness was to be seen in the lack of a self-supporting arrangement for the wide bonnet top; and even worse was the provision of only an external bonnet release.

Externally, a simple grille of horizontal bars in a painted finish easily identified the standard model Cortina. The De Luxe car had a bright metal mesh grille of similar outline, and both cars featured bright screen rubber inserts, chrome plated bumpers, hubcaps, and door handles. Additionally on the De Luxe were bright metal headlamp surrounds, and a similarly bright capping applied to the roof drip rail. There were only eight single colours, with six two-tone combinations available at extra cost. Even without the extra trimmings of the De Luxe, which in any case were tastefully applied, the standard model looked extremely smart as the three-box bodyshell's proportions were exactly right, and very neatly highlighted by discreet panelwork fluting which gave a long low look to the car.

New 4-door Cortina makes the difference bigger still

Ford

4-DOOR MODEL FROM £591.8.9 (tax paid)

CONSUL
CORTINA

The small car with a big difference!

As was to be expected, the power unit for the Cortina was another variation of the engine first seen in the Anglia in 1959, and of course retaining the 81 mm bore, but now with a crankshaft stroke of 58.17 mm giving a capacity of 1198 cc. Copper-lead was now used for the big-end shells and those of the three main bearings also. With a compression ratio of 8.7:1, and a single Solex accelerator-pump type carburettor the engine developed 48.5 bhp nett at 4800 rpm, with the peak of the torque curve occurring at 2700 rpm at which 63 lbs/ft was developed.

The same 7$\frac{1}{2}$ inch diameter clutch as on the Anglia and Classic was retained, but rather than the Anglia's gearbox with its unsynchronised first gear, which would have been no surprise on a new inexpensive model, the Cortina featured the all synchromesh gearbox as first seen on the Classic 1500. A floor mounted gearchange was standard, but inclusive with the bench front seat option was a steering column mounted arrangement. An interesting feature of this gearchange was that the gear selectors were operated by cables running from the base of the steering column to the gearbox. Of a heavy-duty type, these cables were each encased in a lubricated and sealed weatherproof sleeve, and being accurately adjusted in manufacture required no further attention between transmission overhauls; an advantage of these was that no separate left- or right-hand linkages were required to suit left- or right-hand-drive models. Completing the transmission was the usual open propeller shaft to the hypoid-bevel final-drive assembly with its 4.125:1 ratio again as on the Anglia/Classic models. As the Cortina was sharing the Anglia tyre size also, the overall gearing was the same at 16 mph/1000 rpm.

The running gear naturally included Ford's MacPherson strut independent front end set-up, but with slight internal differences in the struts designed to improve their rigidity when well extended. The Ford/Burman recirculating ball steering box had a ratio of 15:1 which, on a system renowned for its lightness, seemed unnecessarily low geared for this relatively lightweight car. The live rear axle was mounted forward of the centre of the longitudinal half-elliptic leaf springs, and a change from usual Ford practice at this end of the car was the appearance of telescopic dampers; these were mounted vertically, ahead of the axle and immediately above the springs.

A Girling all drum braking system was chosen on the grounds of low first cost, and was of just about ample proportions for this size of car with the 8 inch diameter drums at the front housing $1^3/4$ inch width shoes, whilst those at the rear of similar diameter had shoes of $1^1/4$ inches wide, giving a total lining area of 81.6 square inches. Like that of the clutch, the pendant brake pedal operated a master cylinder high up on the bulkhead as pioneered by Ford in Britain with their first Consul in 1950. The 13 inch roadwheels were of 4 inch width and four-stud fixing; being equipped only with 5.20 x 13 tyres, the combination looked a little too skinny on the relatively large Cortina.

Upon their release in September 1962 only the two-door models were immediately available, with four-door production scheduled to begin in November. At £639 and £666 for the standard and De Luxe two-door cars the Cortina was indeed the outstanding value for money its makers had intended it to be. £17/3s/9d had to be added for the heater, and a very reasonable £13/15s/0d if the bench seat/column gearchange layout was required. On the two-door car the front bench seat featured a divided backrest of which each side could be folded forward to ease entry to the rear compartment.

On the road, the Cortina could exceed 75 mph, and accelerate from rest to 60 mph in around 23 seconds. Its fuel consumption was unlikely to be any heavier than 30 mpg under hard driving, whilst better than 40 mpg was being returned at a constant speed of 50 mph. Handling qualities set very high standards, with the very accurately worked out location of the rigid rear axle on the leaf springs virtually eliminating the shortcomings sometimes associated with this conventional system.

By the time the four-door models appeared towards the end of the year an Autumn budget had lowered car prices generally with a reduction in purchase tax, and the full Cortina range was now listed at £573 (2-door), £597 (2-door De Luxe), £591 (4-door) and £615 for the four-door De Luxe car. At these prices it was difficult to categorise the Cortina; this combination of performance, fuel economy, spaciousness, and style, simply wasn't available elsewhere at anything like the price.

With an obvious winner on their hands, Ford naturally developed the Cortina theme to the full, and in January 1963 the Cortina Super appeared. This went considerably further up the ladder of luxury than did the De Luxe

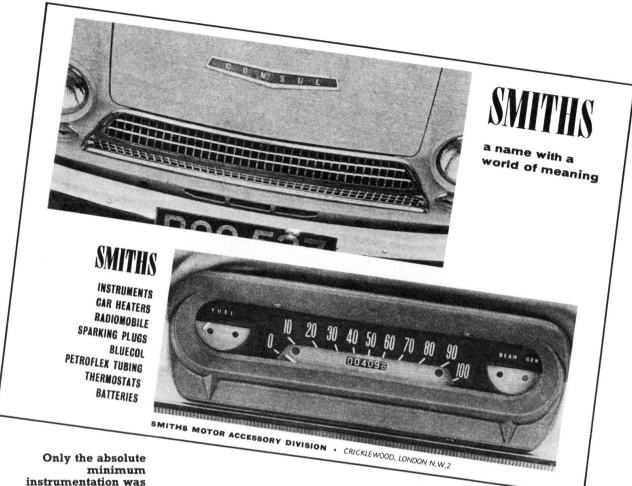

Only the absolute minimum instrumentation was provided, as seen here in a Smiths Industries advertisement which also gives a close-up of the Cortina's front end complete with that rather confusing "Consul" badge.

Cortinas, with its own exclusive seating including a roll front edge, a fully carpeted interior, and the heater and screenwashers as standard equipment. Externally were chrome cappings highlighting the body flutes, a similar finish to the door window frames, and the new Zodiac wheeltrims, whilst the dual tone paint schemes could be specified at no extra charge. A mechanical difference was the inclusion of the 1498 cc engine so far seen only in the Classic, and with this now being accompanied by a 3.9:1 axle ratio on the Cortina Super. With this axle, and larger, 5.60 x 13 tyres, the gearing was raised to a figure of 17.4 mph/1000 rpm which promised more-relaxed high-speed cruising capabilities.

This Cortina possessed a standstill to 60 mph capability of less than 20 seconds, and would just exceed 80 mph flat-out. In part due to the raised gearing, the fuel economy was only slightly impaired, and touring figures in the 30 to 35 mpg range were easily attained. Having put on a little bit of weight in addition to acquiring a greater speed potential, the Super was equipped with a revised all drum braking system which now included 9 inch diameter drums at the front. As all of this was available for £670 (2-door) and £688 the Cortina Super was continuing the value-for-money theme. A "1500" package, comprising the larger engine, brakes, and higher axle ratio, was being made available on the lesser Cortinas for just over £30.

Two months later saw the introduction of the Cortina Estate cars, in either De Luxe 1200 guise at £683, at which it was marginally the cheapest four-door estate car in Britain, or as the Cortina Super estate car at £783. A nicely raked rear end, and slim pillars resulted in a good-looking load carrier which had a maximum load length of 6 feet 5 inches; access to this was via a lift-up tailgate which was counterbalanced and raised to a height which allowed six-footers to load without stooping low. Lever-arm shock absorbers replaced the saloon's telescopics at the rear, and to assist the

engine on the 1200 models a lower axle ratio of 4.444:1 was adopted. This in fact only compensated for the larger tyres – 6.00 x 13 – fitted to the estate car, and which would have raised the gearing by an unreasonable amount for the small engine. These tyres on the Super resulted in 17.8 mph/1000 rpm in conjunction with its unchanged final-drive ratio. A chrome surround to the body fluting identified the De Luxe, whilst the Super estate car was instantly recognisable with its imitation timber framework/wood panelling, and which was not to everyone's taste.

The now legendary Lotus Cortina had made its appearance in January

A revised grille, "Aeroflow" ventilation, and at last a proper Cortina nameplate appeared at Motor Show time in 1964. The ventilation outlets can be seen on the rear quarter pillars in this view from the Ford archives.

94

The extra brightwork seen in these two views signify the Cortina Super, seen here in both two- and four-door form, and amply portraying the Cortina's perfectly balanced lines.

1963, but this was a very specialized, and expensive car, far removed from the family runabout. Much more attractive to the low-budget enthusiast fancying a sportscar but finding a roomy saloon was essential, came the Cortina GT in April 1963.

The heart of the GT was the considerably uprated 1498 cc engine which had made its debut one month earlier in the Consul Capri GT coupe. A modified cylinder head was fitted, raising the compression ratio to 9.0:1, and featuring larger exhaust valves. A revised camshaft gave a small increase in lift, and appreciably longer valve opening periods. A Weber two-stage progressive-choke (compound) carburettor was fitted on a new inlet manifold, and there was a new four-branch exhaust manifold feeding into a large-bore single pipe. In this guise the engine developed 78 bhp nett at 5200 rpm, with a peak torque figure of 91 lbs/ft occurring relatively high up the range at 3600 rpm. Copper-lead main bearing shells, and stronger "Heplex" pistons were changes included to maintain reliability with these higher outputs. Stronger clutch springs were fitted, and the gearbox received a short remote control change lever; the ratios remained the same, as did the 3.9:1 axle of the ordinary 1500 models. A thicker diameter propeller shaft was introduced to ensure lack of vibration at the higher speeds the GT would achieve. Stiffer rate springs, and 5.60 x 13 tyres were fitted, and the anti-roll bar was thicker than on the standard Cortinas, but perhaps the most important running gear change was the adoption of a front disc/rear drum braking system of identical dimensions as on the Ford Classic.

The bodyshell differed from the regular home-market models in that it was based on the thicker floorpan as used on export Cortinas, and as a result the GT would weigh about 1 cwt extra. Inside, the GT was almost identical to the De Luxe specification, but with the addition of a small central console containing an ammeter and oil pressure gauge. An engine temperature gauge filled the vacant spot to the right of the speedometer, and an electronic rev-counter was mounted on the steering column.

Able to accelerate from rest to 60, 70 and 80 mph in around 13, 19, and 26 seconds, the GT would also attain speeds very close to 95 mph. These figures put it well to the fore in the inexpensive performance-saloon class, and at £748 and £766 for the two- and four-door models it recruited many buyers. Its performance on the road was to be matched by a string of competition successes from local club events to top level international rallies. This aspect of the Cortina's career has been well recorded elsewhere; the highlights were many, and were to include outright victory in the East African Safari Rally in 1964.

A Ford photograph of a Cortina estate car which appears to be a development car as it features the mock wood sidetrim of the early Cortina estates, but which was apparently deleted from production models at about the same time aeroflow ventilation, also shown here, was introduced. The excellent carrying capacity of these Cortinas is readily apparent here, as are such details as the tailgate's lower locating tabs which ensure rigidity is maintained.

Just as useful of course without the extra trim, this estate car reveals the frontal treatment which remained exactly as on the saloons.

September 1963 saw the introduction of a revised instrument layout with the stylised speedometer giving way to an arrangement in which twin circular dials appeared in a neat panel brought forward from the facia over the steering column. A new item of optional equipment now on the 1500 Cortinas (except the GT) was the Borg Warner Model 35 automatic transmission, and which added £82 to the price when specified. This proved to be extremely well matched to this particular Ford engine, with Cortinas so equipped showing only very little inferiority in terms of sheer performance, whilst admittedly using rather more fuel than the manual versions under give and take road conditions.

Considerable revisions were introduced in October 1964, with the most noticeable of these being the aeroflow ventilation system. This, with its facia "eyeball" vents, and extractors in the rear quarter pillars could be set to admit either warm or cool air into the interior and completely change the air every 40 seconds. A restyled facia panel, again housing circular instruments, had a rather more expensive look about it as did a new three-spoked steering wheel; a nylon cloth upholstery option was also new. Changes under the skin were a slight increase in compression ratios on both 1200 and 1500 engines, although with no quoted power output improvements, disc brakes at the front standardized throughout the range, and improved rear axle location on the GT. The latter consisted of radius arms running forward from the axle to attachment points on the inside face of the longitudinal underfloor members.

Identifying these latest Cortinas were an attractive new grille of finer mesh and, at last, the name Cortina replacing the mis-leading Consul badge which had so far occupied a prominent position on the bonnet front.

The excellent aeroflow ventilation rendered the front swivelling quarter windows superflous, and the deletion of these was one of the few changes to be seen from September 1965. The steering column gearchange option was also withdrawn now; and interestingly, the standard model 1200 Cortinas could now only be supplied to special order as virtually all buyers were opting for the De Luxe and Super cars. The Super estate car now lost the imitation woodwork, with this being replaced by the simpler chrome mouldings and a two-tone paint scheme. With these small revisions the Cortina range continued for another year as Britain's fastest-selling car on a worldwide basis, reaching the magic one million production figure in record-breaking time during 1966, before being replaced in October of that year by the new Cortina Mk 2 range.

Datapanel: Ford Cortina 1200, 1500, 1500 GT.

	1200	1500 (1500 GT)
Engine	4 cyl, ohv	4 cyl, ohv
Capacity	1198 cc	1498 cc
Bore	80.96 mm	80.96 mm
Stroke	58.17 mm	72.75 mm
Compression ratio	8.7:1	8.3:1 (9.0:1)
Max BHP	48.5 nett @ 4800 rpm	59.5 nett @ 4600 rpm (78 nett @ 5200 rpm)
Max torque	63 lbs/ft @ 2700 rpm	81.5 lbs/ft @ 2300 rpm (91 lbs/ft @ 3600 rpm)
Gearing	16 mph/1000 rpm	17.4 mph/1000 rpm
Tyres	5.20 x 13	5.60 x 13
Kerb weight	16 cwt	16$^{1}/_{4}$ cwt (17$^{1}/_{2}$ cwt)
Overall length	14 ft 2 in	14 ft 2 in
Overall width	5 ft 3 in	5 ft 3 in
Wheelbase	8 ft 2 in	8 ft 2 in
Performance	"Autocar" 28th September 1962 (2-door De Luxe)	"Autocar" 25th January 1963 (4-door Super)
Max speed		
Top gear	76.5 mph (mean) 77.0 mph (best)	80.8 mph (mean) 82.0 mph (best)
3rd gear	69 mph	73 mph
2nd gear	41 mph	43 mph
1st gear	27 mph	29 mph
Acceleration		
0–30 mph	5.6 seconds	4.9 seconds
0–50 mph	14.8 seconds	12.8 seconds
0–60 mph	22.5 seconds	19.0 seconds
0–70 mph	37.3 seconds	33.2 seconds
	Top gear/3rd gear	Top gear/3rd gear
20–40 mph	12.8/7.8 seconds	10.5/7.3 seconds
30–50 mph	13.1/9.5 seconds	11.2/8.2 seconds
40–60 mph	15.4/12.3 seconds	12.7/10.2 seconds
50–70 mph	24.5/– seconds	20.6/18.9 seconds
Fuel consumption	30.2 mpg (1430 miles)	27.2 mpg (1325 miles)

During the development of the Cortina it became obvious that by comparison the Classic was an unecessarily expensive to produce car for its market sector, which was only a little further up the scale; that fact having been accepted there was little point in keeping the Classic in production even though it was a relative newcomer on the scene. It was however gathering a useful following from people to whom the Cortina might appear a little too down-market, and therefore a replacement for the Classic, in all its manifestations, was considered valid, and therefore development of yet another new car was quickly under way.

The basis for the new two- and four-door bodyshell was to be the Cortina's floorpan, albeit double-skinned in parts this time, and with the important difference that it would be lengthened by 3 inches; this was achieved by inserting an extra section in the floor just ahead of the rear wheelarches. The wheelbase was therefore lengthened by the same amount, to 8 feet 5 inches, whilst suitably longer front and rear body sections resulting in an overall length now of 14 feet 9 inches maintained the correct visual proportions.

Front inner wings, now longer ahead of the suspension mountings, were otherwise as those of the Cortina, as was also the front scuttle/bulkhead area and windscreen pillars. Although a completely new bonnet top was necessary to follow the front end styling, details such as the bonnet hinges and the simple support strut were the same, but the bonnet release was now thankfully back where it should be – inside the car. The window frames forming the upper part of the doors followed the Cortina pattern, but the roof of the Corsair was slightly higher, and much broader rear quarter pillars were to be seen. Outer panelwork below the shoulder line was all new, and so completed a transformation in appearance which was such as to give very little hint that this new car was quite substantially a re-skinned Cortina.

The overall styling, although not so controversial as on the superseded

A replacement for the Classic, but in fact a derivative of the Cortina, the new Consul Corsair was indeed an elegant car just as is suggested in this brochure reproduction.

With perhaps as many as 400 years separating their birth, the Tudor House and Ford Corsair nevertheless combine to make a lovely picture.

This time in the studio, another Corsair displays those elegant lines. The additional chrome side trim, and just visible rear wing badge indicate that this is the high-performance Corsair GT.

Consul Classic, was nevertheless quite individual enough with its almost cigar like shape beneath the shoulder line to render the Corsair instantly recognisable. There was more than just a hint of the much larger American Ford Thunderbird in this shape which rather surprisingly lent itself well to the smaller dimensions of this British Ford. Stylized chrome-plated bumpers blended in well to the car's shape at their extremities, and the integration of the headlamps, and the sidelamps and direction indicators at both ends of the car was very neatly carried out. As on the Classic and the Zephyr range the rear number plate concealed the fuel filler cap.

Like the Classic which it was to replace, and therefore unlike the Cortina from which it was derived, the Corsair was not intended to be a bargain-basement model in the medium sector, and so at the design stage quite considerable attention was paid to the suppression of noise and vibration. The double skinning of certain areas of the floorpan and transmission tunnel helped in this respect, and there was both plastic foam and felt beneath the carpets, and glass fibre insulation for the engine compartment bulkhead.

Principally for some expert territories where utilitarian trim was still considered an advantage, a standard model was being produced, but for Britain and those other world markets where some luxury is appreciated the well-appointed De Luxe Corsairs would be in effect "standard" models. On these, as with the cheaper versions, the front bench seat and column gearchange were the normal equipment, but only a small extra charge would buy individual front seats and Ford's excellent remote control floor gearshift. High quality Cirrus or Ambla PVC was used for the seat coverings and trim, with quite elaborate patterns on both seats and doors; single or dual tone trim could be specified. All doors were equipped with a combined armrest/doorpull, but armrests were a surprising omission in the rear of the two-door cars. Loop-pile carpeting covered the floor, and Ford's usual light-coloured washable vinyl roof lining was to be seen again.

The twin sunvisors were of the crushable type, and a thickly padded leading edge was a prominent feature of the facia layout. Placed above this

The supplementary instruments on the central console, and the column mounted rev counter also indicate a GT model. The stylised hornring – or is it a hornoblong? – did unfortunately tend to obscure the speedometer for some Corsair drivers, and was replaced on later models.

to the offside was a rectangular panel, with a matching panel beneath. Housed in the upper panel were an elongated speedometer and gauges for the fuel level and engine temperature, with these being in front of the driver; and to their left the heater controls, cigarette lighter and ashtray. Provision for the optional radio was included in the lower panel. Obviating the mass of wiring normally to be found behind the dashboard, the instrument panel was the first on a British car to be of the printed circuit type. This was connected to the main wiring loom by just one plug, with the 13 pin connector being so arranged that it could not be wrongly plugged in. Controls for the lights and direction indicators sprouted from the steering column in such close proximity as to sometimes cause confusion, whereas in contrast the other minor controls were sensibly situated about the facia panel well apart from each other. The electric wipers were of variable speed operation, and windscreen washers were provided; the heater, however, still remained an extra cost item.

A hornring of oblong shape adorned the steering wheel, and seemed to have been designed specifically to obscure the speedometer when the wheel was in the straight-ahead position. Surprisingly, the two-spoke steering wheel was of flat design, but padding was to be seen across its centre. Ahead of the passenger was a lidded compartment, and running full width beneath the facia was a parcel shelf complete with padded leading edge.

The mechanical elements were virtually those of the Classic and Cortina Super, with the 3.9:1 axle ratio of the latter now being used rather than the lower gearing of the Classic. Power and torque outputs of the 1½ litre five main bearing engine were unaltered, as were the gearbox ratios, but there were unseen changes comprising thicker internal webs in the engine/gearbox castings. These were introduced to improve the mechanical refinement by stiffening up these parts (so benefiting the 1500 Cortina also), as was a larger diameter propeller shaft for the Corsair to further reduce driveline vibration. The running gear differed only from the preceding Classic in that the lever-arm shock absorbers now gave way to the telescopic type as on the Cortina.

The redesigned steering wheel removed the earlier objections. The column-mounted gear selector for the optional automatic transmission can just be seen in this view.

The success of the Cortina GT suggested that a similar version of the Corsair would be well received, and so with this variation added the new model was to offer a wider choice than had the Classic. The engine, gearbox, and rear axle for the Corsair GT were exactly as on the respective Cortina, but as the Corsair was slightly heavier than that car it was to have the benefit of vacuum servo assistance for the otherwise unchanged Girling front disc/rear drum braking system. A higher geared steering box, revised damper settings, and stiffer front springs were other differences between the GT and normal Corsairs. A rev-counter on the steering column, ammeter and oil pressure gauges in a central console, and a padded armrest which could be lifted to reveal a small stowage compartment between the individual front seats were all GT items as seen already on the GT Cortina. Externally, small GT shields on the rear flanks, and a chrome moulding along the sills and wing bottoms in addition to the one at shoulder level on the normal Corsairs were all that identified this high-performance Corsair.

The very careful planning had produced a car which was a worthy successor to the Classic, and which in fact offered definite improvements in respect of refinement of running; but in which also savings of around 1 cwt of raw materials had been achieved, thus making the Corsair a usefully less

103

expensive car to produce as had been the intention. In view of this the development costs could be quickly recouped without the necessity of increased prices, and so when the Corsair made its appearance in October 1963 it was at the same attractive levels as the outgoing Classic, which itself had benefited from purchase tax reductions since its announcement. Prices of £653 (2-door standard), £677 (4-door standard/2-door De Luxe), and £701 for the four-door De Luxe were being asked; the heater unit was £15/2s/1d

Datapanel: Ford Consul Corsair, Corsair GT.

	Corsair	Corsair GT
Engine	4 cyl, ohv	4 cyl, ohv
Capacity	1498 cc	1498 cc
Bore	80.96 mm	80.96 mm
Stroke	72.75 mm	72.75 mm
Compression ratio	8.3:1	9.0:1
Max BHP	59.5 nett @ 4600 rpm	78 nett @ 5200 rpm
Max torque	81.5 lbs/ft @ 2300 rpm	91 lbs/ft @ 3600 rpm
Gearing	17.4 mph/1000 rpm	17.4 mph/1000 rpm
Tyres	5.60 x 13	5.60 x 13
Kerb weight	17$\frac{1}{2}$ cwt	18 cwt
Overall length	14 ft 9 in	14 ft 9 in
Overall width	5 ft 3$\frac{1}{2}$ in	5 ft 3$\frac{1}{2}$ in
Wheelbase	8 ft 5 in	8 ft 5 in
Performance		
	"The Motor" R/T No. 38/63 (4-door De Luxe)	"The Motor" R/T No. 5/65 (4-door)
Max speed		
Top gear	83.8 mph (mean) 85.0 mph (best)	92.1 mph (mean) 92.8 mph (best)
3rd gear	76 mph	75 mph
2nd gear	48 mph	51 mph
1st gear	33 mph	28 mph
Acceleration		
0–30 mph	5.1 seconds	3.4 seconds
0–50 mph	13.6 seconds	8.9 seconds
0–60 mph	19.0 seconds	12.8 seconds
0–70 mph	29.7 seconds	19.0 seconds
0–80 mph	–	30.2 seconds
	Top gear/3rd gear	Top gear/3rd gear
20–40 mph	11.1/7.2 seconds	10.2/6.1 seconds
30–50 mph	10.6/8.1 seconds	9.9/6.5 seconds
40–60 mph	12.0/9.3 seconds	11.4/7.1 seconds
50–70 mph	17.3/16.6 seconds	13.8/9.4 seconds
60–80 mph	–/–	16.9/– seconds
Fuel consumption	26.0 mpg (1069 miles)	29.0 mpg (1790 miles)

extra, whilst a further £8/9s/2d was needed if the individual front seats were ordered. Both these items were standard equipment on the Corsair GT for which £816 (2-door) and £840 was charged.

With a little less weight to pull than the Classic, the Corsair was a livelier car except at the bottom end of the range in top and third gears, where its higher overall gearing lessened the acceleration somewhat; that gearing, however, and the clean shape, enabled the Corsair to comfortably exceed the 80 mph mark, and return generally better fuel consumption figures. The performance of the GT included a maximum in excess of 90 mph, and acceleration only very slightly inferior to that of the lighter Cortina GT. Interestingly, with its streamlined body allied to the high-efficiency GT engine, the Corsair GT proved to be the most economical of all the $1^1/2$ litre Classic/Cortina/Corsair saloons under hard-driving conditions.

At its price and performance levels, the Corsair's closest rivals were Vauxhall's successful FB Victor and VX 4/90 range, at £635 (basic), £667 (Super), and £723 for the Victor De Luxe; the high-performance VX 4/90 matched the corresponding Corsair GT exactly, at £840.

Within a month or so of going into production the driver's seat in the Corsairs was given a further inch of rearward adjustment, which had little effect on the excellent rear compartment knee-room, but did go some way towards answering comments from some that tall drivers sat too close to the steering wheel. Quickly gaining widespread public approval, the Corsair was soon leaving the company's new Halewood assembly plant at the planned maximum rate of 500 cars per day, but at which it still proved unable to meet the demand throughout 1964, during which some buyers were spending up to twelve weeks on the waiting list.

A new, dished steering wheel, with three spokes and lower-half hornring made its appearance in October 1964 along with other slight changes. These included a new multi-purpose stalk replacing the lights/indicator switchgear on the steering column, and, on the GT, the rev-counter now placed in the central console in the position vacated by the small supplementary instruments which were now occupying a space in the upper facia panel. Radius arms providing additional location for the rear axle were also now to be found on the GT, keeping it in line with the similarly improved GT Cortina.

In this form the Corsairs were to continue for just one more year, after which they were superseded by the similarly bodied models which featured Ford's all-new V4-cylinder engines and several other changes.

3

HILLMAN

SUPER MINX Making its appearance in October 1961, the Super Minx was an addition to the Rootes Group's well-established Hillman Minx models which were to continue in production alongside the new car. Aimed rather more up market than the existing Minx, the Super Minx was only a slightly larger car externally, at 13 feet 9 inches long and 5 feet 2½ inches wide being just 3

**ROOTES
stands superb at every show**

The brilliant new
HILLMAN SUPER MINX

A pleasing artist's impression serves to advertise the new Super Minx at Motor Show time.

inches longer and 2 inches wider than the Minx, but in which appreciably more interior space was being provided as a result of careful attention being paid to maximising interior room within a conventional layout. Therefore, the wheelbase was increased by 5 inches by comparison with that of the ordinary Minx, to 8 feet 5 inches, of which four of the extra inches were behind the dashboard line, and 13 inch diameter roadwheels replaced the 15 inch variety, thus eliminating wheelarch intrusion into what was already a larger passenger compartment.

Of conventional monocoque construction, the four-door bodyshell was well braced underneath with a front pair of longitudinal U-section members terminating under the front seating position where they met with a sturdy transverse member. Similar rear end members ran forward to the rear compartment heelboard, whilst also aiding overall rigidity were box-section inner sills and welded up front wings. The full-width bonnet top was counterbalanced, thus making it much more convenient than most in this class of car, and another good feature was to be seen in the thick covering of sound-deadening material on the engine side of the scuttle/bulkhead structure. Styling considerations had resulted in a quite pronounced wrap-around front screen, but the pillar angle had been carefully worked out so as not to seriously intrude into the front door gap, and in fact ease of entry to the front compartment was good for this size of car, as indeed it was too at the rear. Also very convenient, the counterbalanced boot lid opened from boot floor level, and revealed a usefully-shaped compartment; the 11 gallon fuel tank mounted transversely behind the rear seat bulkhead did occupy quite considerable space, but the spare wheel had been located in a drop-down tray beneath the compartment, thus leaving an uninterrupted flat floor. A rexine covering extended to include the fuel tank, above which there was room for stowage of smallish soft items.

Neat, and nicely finished interior appointments had characterized successive generations of Hillmans, and the Super Minx was to be no exception to this worthy tradition. Interestingly, there was just one trim and equipment level at the list price, with this level approximating to something nearer the deluxe standards which applied at that time when basic and de luxe versions of many family saloons were usually available. Thick carpeting covered the floor, with the seating and door trims being covered in ICI's Vynide PVC material. A rather simple, close-set pleated design was used for the seats, and was sufficiently ribbed to provide some sideways location on the bench seating which was standard and devoid of central armrests; individual front seats were to be available at extra cost. Armrests were also omitted from the doors, with these being closed by means of chromed pulls situated on the door window sill; swivelling quarter windows in addition to the main drop windows were a feature of the front doors, whilst only the main door windows opened in the rear.

The dished steering wheel was of two-spoke design, and complete with a full-circle hornring. Viewed through this were two large circular dials, and a smaller one in between. A speedometer filled the left-hand dial, with that in the middle housing the fuel gauge, whilst in the right-hand side one a temperature gauge occupied one third leaving two vacant spaces for the ammeter and oil pressure gauge which were optional extras. A Rootes medallion in a central position on the facia concealed an aperture designed to accommodate an electric clock which was also to be available at extra cost. Flanking the clock position at each side were the controls for the heating and demisting unit which was welcome standard equipment, as was also a windscreen washer. A usefully sized lockable glove box on the passenger side had its lid neatly styled into the facia panel; the facia top was well padded, as was the front edge of the lower parcel shelf running the full width of the car.

Well balanced, and with the wrap-around front and rear screen pillars, and the mildly finned rear wings playing their part well in the overall styling, the three-box bodyshell required only discreet bright metal embellishments. A narrow, full length chrome strip, running at waist height, effectively broke up the expanse of the body sides; the plain bumper bars were without overriders, although the latter could be specified at extra cost, whilst the simple horizontal front grille was relieved only by a small central badge. Five single, and five extra cost two-colour schemes were available, with the second colour of the dual tone finishes being confined to the roof and rear pillars.

The power unit was the 1.6 litre four-cylinder engine which was also powering the Minx 111C. This engine had first appeared late in 1954 as a 1390 cc, 76 mm x 76 mm unit, and had subsequently been enlarged to 1494 cc (79 mm bore) in 1958, and then to 1592 cc earlier in 1961 by virtue of a further increase in bore size to 81.5 mm. In the Super Minx installation it differed slightly from that of the Minx 111C in that it developed the greater horsepower deemed necessary to now propel the heavier Super Minx. This was achieved largely by adopting a different camshaft profile which gave greater overlap, and revised settings for the Zenith carburettor. The compression ratio remained the same at 8.3:1, and in this form 62 bhp at 4800 rpm was developed (52 bhp @ 4100 rpm, Minx 111C), but at the expense of the peak torque figure which was down slightly to 84.4 lbs/ft at 2800 rpm (86.8 lbs/ft @ 2100 rpm, Minx 111C). This suggested a rather less flexible unit than on the smaller Minx, but this would be compensated for somewhat by the lower overall gearing which resulted from the Super Minx's smaller roadwheels.

Convertible Plus!
the family car with the fresh sporting air

New HILLMAN Super Minx Convertible

This is the new Hillman Super Minx Convertible ... the Convertible *plus*. Take a good look at it. *Plus one*—the extra structural strength that gives saloon car stability. *Plus two*—the snug-fitting hood to keep you saloon-car-cosy in all weathers. *Plus three*—the smart acceleration and over 80 m.p.h. from the proven 1·6 litre engine (backed by smooth, progressive braking to match). *Plus four*—the styling: the crisp, clean lines of the car that excite admiration wherever you go. *Plus five*—the host of extra features. Like the built-in heater. The screen-washers. The padded facia and safety belt anchor points. *And plus six*—a sensible price. Hillman value has never been so good.

£698 plus p.t. £262.15.3
Fully-automatic transmission, white-wall tyres and over-riders are available as extras

6709 HP

A PRODUCT OF **ROOTES MOTORS LIMITED**

HILLMAN MOTOR CAR COMPANY LIMITED · DIVISION OF ROOTES MOTORS LIMITED · LONDON SHOWROOMS & EXPORT DIVISION: ROOTES LIMITED · DEVONSHIRE HOUSE · PICCADILLY · LONDON W.1

The four-speed gearbox was still without synchronization for first gear, and was controlled by a short floor mounted lever which was close enough to the standard front bench seat to make three-abreast seating difficult; curiously, a column change option was only available on the export cars. An interesting feature of the driveline was a new propeller shaft rear universal coupling by Metalastik, which included bonded rubber ball joints for the universal action and eliminated the usual needle roller bearings. The 4.22:1 axle ratio in conjunction with the 13 inch roadwheels gave 16.2 mph/1000 rpm on top gear. An alternative transmission available at extra cost was the Smiths "Easidrive" three-speed automatic gearbox first seen in late 1959 on the Minx 111A, and unique with its magnetic couplings in place of the more usual torque converter.

The running gear followed the established Minx pattern, with coil spring and double wishbone independent front suspension units; a stiffer anti-roll

bar than before now linked these units. Burman recirculating ball steering gear was employed, with the steering box and track rods etc. in the safety position behind the axle line. Of five leaves each were a pair of longitudinally mounted semi-elliptics locating the back axle, with the suspension arrangements being completed by telescopic dampers all round. The Lockheed hydraulic drum braking system comprised 9 inch diameter drums, and shoes with a total lining area of 121 square inches. The tyres were a sensibly-sized 5.90 x 13.

Priced at £854 upon its introduction (October 1961), The Super Minx was faced with the Austin A60 Cambridge De Luxe at £884, the Vauxhall Victor FB De Luxe at £847, and the Ford Classic at £825 in its four-door De Luxe configuration. The Hillman's passenger carrying capacity very closely matched these rivals, whilst in terms of overall performance it was a near enough match for the Austin, whilst being superior to the Ford and Vauxhall, and particularly so at the top end where it would continue to a maximum speed of over 80 mph. Whilst if used to the full its extra performance would result in poorer fuel consumption than its rivals, under normal touring conditions it would not be significantly worse, and a cross-country 30 mpg was within reach if leisurely progress would suffice.

Obviously, this new Hillman was a strong contender in its class, and it was most unfortunate that a strike delayed its production soon after it was announced. By early 1962 however production was building up, and first in April came the addition of a Super Minx estate car, to be followed in July by the introduction of a two-door convertible model. The estate car retained the four passenger door layout, but with the window frames of the rear pair being squared up. Very slim rear pillars maintained the excellent all round vision which was such a good feature of the saloon. The new rear side windows were fixed, and across the back was a horizontally-split tailgate of which the upper half was self-supporting when open. From the centre pillar rearwards the new roof was strengthened by being of an attractive-looking transverse-ribbed design, and with the retention of the saloon's rear wing/fin design the overall effect was good. Increased spring rates to cater for the heavier loads were the only technical changes.

In its convertible configuration the Super Minx looked most attractive. Manually operated, the hood was of neat design when raised, and featured a larger than usual rear window by convertible standards. Unfortunately there was no De Ville (half way) position as on previous convertibles, but fully retractable rear quarter windows, and of course the usual wind-down door windows still gave scope for several different arrangements. Individual front seats with folding squabs allowed reasonably good access to a rear compartment somewhat narrower than the saloon due to the hood mechanism. Compensating for the lack of a steel roof was additional X-bracing welded into the underside of the floorpan.

Purchase tax reductions in the April budget had resulted in the saloon now being listed at £805, with the estate car and convertible making their debut at £888 and £960 respectively.

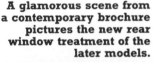

A glamorous scene from a contemporary brochure pictures the new rear window treatment of the later models.

Several changes to the range were announced in October 1962, and were considered sufficient to now designate the model as the Mk 2. A Solex carburettor replaced the Zenith, and was in conjunction with a new camshaft which reduced the valve overlap slightly and improved the peak torque output, but at the slight expense of maximum bhp. However, both maximum outputs were now developed at usefully lower rpm, with figures of 58 bhp at 4400 rpm, and 86.3 lbs/ft at 2500 rpm now indicating an altogether more flexible engine. A new axle ratio of 3.89:1 accompanied the revised engine, giving 17.2 mph/1000 rpm, and all of this added up to an overall performance about the same as before, but achieved in a more effortless manner and with better constant-speed fuel economy. Bearing in mind their load carrying capabilities, the estate cars retained the 4.22:1 axle. Another change now was that, when specified, the automatic gearbox option would be the Borg Warner Model 35. Although remaining without power assistance, the braking arrangements now included 10.3 inch diameter discs for the front wheels in place of the previous drums.

The front bench seat was deleted, with a new design of individual front seat being standardized. These featured moulded foam squabs and cushions placed over rubber diaphragms, and were claimed to more accurately adopt the shape of the occupant. A new fuel tank, of $10^1/_2$ gallon capacity, now occupied a position inside the left-hand rear wing recess, giving a slight overall improvement in luggage space.

Prices continued to fall generally, and early in 1963 the Super Minx range was down to £743, £804, and £843, for the saloon, estate car, and convertible models respectively. At this level the saloon was looking good enough between such as the Austin A60 De Luxe at £755, and the appropriate Vauxhall Victor and Ford Classic each at £701.

A slight change came in late 1963 when the Super Minx saloon and convertible re-adopted the 4.22:1 axle ratio, thus sharpening up the acceleration a little but at the expense of fuel economy. The convertible was deleted during the summer of 1964, but the good-selling saloon and estate car continued and went into Mk 3 configuration in September that year.

Characterizing the Mk 3 was a major rework of the body above the

A deeper windscreen accompanied the revised rear window line. EKH 855C, a 1965 Mk 3, was caught by the camera when only four years old in 1969 . . .

. . . whereas this well-preserved example of the Super Minx estate car was photographed in more recent times.

shoulder line, with a new and lower roof line squared up rear door pillars, and separate rear quarter windows in conjunction with a new and flatter rear screen replacing the previous wrap-around design. A larger front screen extended upwards to full roof height. Overriders, and polished metal wheeltrims were standardized, and if the dual tone paintwork was specified the second colour now appeared in the narrow space between two chrome strips running the length of the car; single tone cars retained the one chrome strip each side as before. Another external change to be seen on the estate car were longitudinal rather than transverse stiffening ribs on the roof. Inside, the facia now had a matt black finish to its upper half, with a wood veneer finish below giving a more expensive look. New individual

113

SINGER VOGUE ESTATE CAR

It's loaded with luxury features!

Take the luxurious Singer Vogue saloon. Extend the body. Put in fold-flat rear seats. Include a loading platform. Finish off with a tailgate that extends the loading platform to 79 inches. And there you have the new Vogue Estate Car— the latest way to take five adults (or 700 lb. of luggage) for a really comfortable ride. Here are all the features you expect in a quality car — including a complete heating and ventilation system, excellent suspension and sound-proofing, and twin headlights for night-driving safety.

POWERED BY LIVELY, FULLY-PROVED 1·6 LITRE ENGINE
Optional extras: overdrive on 3rd and 4th gears, or fully-automatic transmission. Whitewall tyres.
£705 PLUS P.T. £265-7-9

ALSO THE SINGER VOGUE LUXURY SALOON
£705 PLUS P.T. £265-7-9

A different frontal treatment served to identify the rather more up-market Singer Vogue variant of this sturdy Rootes Group theme.

front seats with fully reclining squabs were fitted, and on the saloon there were now armrests on the doors.

The engine was remaining exactly as before, but a diaphragm-spring clutch was new, as was a completely new gearbox featuring baulk-ring synchromesh on all four forward gears. A price increase for the saloon, to £769, accompanied these improvements, but the estate car had actually fallen in price very slightly to £799. Vauxhall's brand-new Victor 101 De Luxe saloon was £775, and an equivalent Austin A60 Cambridge was £757, so the Super Minx was still very competitive indeed.

The model continued in this form for just another year before further changes were introduced, the principle of which was a further enlargement in engine capacity to 1725 cc. This was achieved by lengthening the stroke, by quite a substantial amount, from 76.2 mm to 82.5 mm, as a significant increase in the bore size now would have sacrificed the desirable water jacketing which had been retained around each individual cylinder. The relatively wide bore centres which had allowed the generous water jacketing did leave room to accommodate an additional, if rather narrow main bearing between cylinders number 1 and 2, and numbers 3 and 4, and so a five main bearing layout was now adopted thus ensuring that the much longer-throw crankshaft remained well supported. With 65 bhp at 4800 rpm,

SINGER

Announce an exciting New Model

Stop, look — and compare. Here is the magnificent new Singer Vogue by Rootes.

MORE POWER — brilliant 1.6 litre engine with high compression aluminium head and other advanced features giving 35% extra power and greater acceleration — with economy. There's also a new compound carburettor to give twin carburettor performance without special tuning.

NEW STYLING — new roofline gives lower, sleeker lines. Deeper windscreen and re-styled window give improved all-round vision.

Attractive range of colours.

NEW COMFORT — individual front seats adjustable to a fully reclining position. Improved suspension and sound insulation.

NEW REFINEMENTS — new all-synchromesh, 4-speed gearbox. New light pressure self-adjusting clutch. Improved handbrake. Dimmable warning lights. Combined windscreen wiper/washer control.

OPTIONAL EXTRAS — *Borg-Warner fully-automatic transmission or Laycock de Normanville Overdrive (top and third gears). Whitewall tyres.*

Saloon £844.19.7 (inc. £146.19.7 p.t.) **Estate Car £900.11.3** (inc. £156.11.3 p.t.)

TEST DRIVE THE EXCITING NEW VOGUE AT YOUR SINGER DEALER

NEW SINGER VOGUE

The revised window lines also appeared on the Singer Vogue late in 1964, and along with other improvements well-documented in this period advertisement.

and 91 lbs/ft of torque at exactly half that number of revolutions, there was a useful increase in acceleration, and for those wishing for a more effortless motorway performance a Laycock de Normanville overdrive was now available at extra cost.

In almost all other respects the Super Minx was as before, and a price increase now to £805 reflected the improved specification of the engine. This was the final phase in the development of the line, with the Super Minx along with several other Rootes Group models giving way to the new "Arrow" range during 1966, of which the Hillman Hunter was the direct Super Minx replacement.

The Upmarket Badge-Engineered Derivatives

Actually appearing nearly three months earlier than the Super Minx, was an

Rootes present...

the superbly equipped

HUMBER SCEPTRE

Humber luxury in a **new** sports saloon!

Never before has there been a car so superbly equipped...
with such a performance ... at so modest a price !

- New self-cancelling overdrive on top and third gears fitted as standard.
- Built-in heating and ventilation.
- High performance 1·6 litre engine, developing 85·5 b.h.p.
- Servo-assisted front disc, rear drum brakes for fade-free braking.
- No greasing points.
- Finest quality coachwork giving maximum strength and safety.

- Richly appointed interior, with roomy individual front seats.
- Wide-opening doors.
- Built-in screenwashers, clock, rev. counter and cigar lighter.
- Generous luggage space in the carpeted boot.

£825 plus p.t. £172.8.9.
Whitewall tyres extra

Appearing early in 1963, the Humber Sceptre was the top-of-the-range model, and as such featured its own exclusive window treatment and lower roof line, but was not in fact of greater width as suggested in this artist's impression!

up-market variation badged as a Singer and with the model name Vogue. The frontal styling differed from that of the Hillman version principally by the use of a traditional-looking upright Singer radiator grille, and the provision of four headlamps. This involved different upper front wing pressings and bonnet top, and gave the car a quite different character when viewed head-on. Bumper overriders were standard, and a different rear lamp cluster was an identification feature at the rear; the full length bright metal moulding running along the side of the car was broader than on the Hillman, and was of a concave design.

TWO WORLDS – ONE CAR

Complete with every refinement for under £1000

One look at the sweeping lines of the Humber Sceptre, one exhilarating drive will tell you that this is a Humber with a very definite place in the sporting world ... but built in the finest tradition of Humber luxury.

HUMBER SCEPTRE
for luxury in a sporting mood

* Rally proved engine gives over 90 m.p.h. with acceleration to match * Self cancelling overdrive on top and third gears * Full instrumentation including rev. counter, water temperature and oil pressure gauges, ammeter, headlamp flasher, panel light dimmer * Full size lock-up glove box with grab rail above * Clock and cigarette lighter * Contoured, adjustable seating * Complete carpeting including the boot * Built-in heating and ventilating system throughout * Servo-assisted brakes, with discs at the front * Cowled twin headlamps * Reversing lamps * Overriders and wheel trim discs * Superbly balanced suspension for leech-like roadholding * No greasing points ... All these are standard at remarkably low price of £997.8.9 (£825 plus p.t. £172.8.9)

Further details from your nearest Rootes Dealer

ROOTES MOTORS LIMITED

HUMBER LIMITED · DIVISION OF ROOTES MOTORS LIMITED
LONDON SHOWROOMS AND EXPORT DIVISION: ROOTES LIMITED
DEVONSHIRE HOUSE · PICCADILLY · LONDON W.1.

Now that's more like it. An accurate illustration of the Sceptre this time shows it to be indeed a handsome car. And just look at all those standard features – for less than £1000!

Although still covered in Vynide as on the Hillman, the Vogue's bench seats were of plushier design but with only that in the front being complete with a pull-down centre armrest; in the rear compartment only, armrests appeared on each door. A walnut facia housed a rectangular speedometer of the moving strip type, and completing the instrumentation were an ammeter and gauges for fuel, engine temperature and oil pressure.

The entire running gear, engine and transmission were as would be seen on the Super Minx, apart from the fact that a Laycock overdrive was

The Sceptre retained its distinctive roof line unchanged throughout its production run, but on becoming the Sceptre Mk 2, late in 1965, received new frontal treatment which in fact utilised the Super Minx wings and bonnet top. Obviously one of the first Mk 2s, FAT 992C was photographed as a seven year old during 1972.

optional on the Singer on which also the engine featured a Solex carburettor rather than the Hillman's Zenith. This had no effect on the quoted power output (62 bhp @ 4800 rpm) but did result in a small increase in the peak torque output to 85.8 lbs/ft at 3000 rpm.

An estate car appeared at the same time as the Hillman estate, but there was no convertible variant of the Singer. The changes in October 1962 already described for the Super Minx also applied to the Vogue, and as the Hillman acquired the Solex carburettor at that time the two models became mechanically identical in their Mk 2 configuration.

In January 1963 a further variant of the design appeared as the Humber Sceptre, and with a similar four headlamp frontal treatment to the Vogue but differing in details such as the Humber grille, and the sidelamp arrangements. A very large, double curvature screen was an instant recognition feature, and from its upper edge the roof line fell rearwards giving a lower line to the Humber than on the Hillman and Singer versions. This feature in fact altered the appearance quite noticeably, and made for what many would say was the best-looking car of this particular Rootes' series. PVC seating was to be found as in the two cheaper cars, but of a design exclusive to the Sceptre, as was its rather sporting steering wheel, and central console from which sprouted a short, gaitered gearlever. Comprehensive instrumentation consisted of two large hooded dials ahead of the driver, and a row of four supplementary dials occupying the centre of a futuristically-styled facia.

Although sharing the same basic 1592 cc four-cylinder engine as the other two cars the Sceptre was the more powerful of the trio as its unit featured the high compression (9.1:1) light-alloy cylinder head, and twin Zenith carburettors to be found on the company's Sunbeam Rapier two-door sports saloon. These features raised the output to 80 bhp at 5200 rpm, and as a result the Sceptre was in the 90 mph class and could reach 60 and 70 mph in around 18 and 25 seconds. The four-speed gearbox was supplemented by the Laycock overdrive as standard equipment, with the Borg Warner Model 35 automatic being available at extra cost. The running gear was as on the latest disc-braked Hillman/Singer versions, and at £998 the Sceptre was an attractive proposition to those seeking a well-finished and quite luxurious car of good performance, but within compact overall dimensions.

Early in 1964 a single Solex twin-choke compound carburettor replaced

Datapanel: Hillman Super Minx

	1592 cc (Mk 1/2/3)	1725 cc (Mk 4)
Engine	4 cyl, ohv	4 cyl, ohv
Capacity	1592 cc	1725 cc
Bore	81.5 mm	81.5 mm
Stroke	76.2 mm	82.5 mm
Compression ratio	8.3:1	8.4:1
Max BHP	62 nett @ 4800 rpm (Mk 1) 58 nett @ 4400 rpm (Mk 2/3)	65 nett @ 4800 rpm
Max torque	84.4 lbs/ft @ 2800 rpm (Mk 1) 86.3 lbs/ft @ 2500 rpm (Mk 2/3)	91.4 lbs/ft @ 2400 rpm
Gearing	16.2 mph/1000 rpm (4.22:1 axle) 17.2 mph/1000 rpm (3.89:1 axle)	17.2 mph/1000 rpm
Tyres	5.90/6.00 x 13	6.00 x 13
Kerb weight	$21^1/4$ cwt	$21^1/4$ cwt
Overall length	13 ft 9 in	13 ft 10 in
Overall width	5 ft $2^1/2$ in	5 ft $2^1/2$ in
Wheelbase	8 ft 5 in	8 ft 5 in
Performance		
	"The Autocar" 23rd March 1962	"Motor" RT No. 13/66 (with overdrive & 4.22 axle)
Max speed		
Top gear	83.1 mph (mean)	82.4 mph (mean) Overdrive
	86.0 mph (best)	86.5 mph (best) Overdrive
3rd gear	68 mph	71 mph
2nd gear	43 mph	46 mph
1st gear	28 mph	30 mph
Acceleration		
0–30 mph	5.7 seconds	4.9 seconds
0–50 mph	14.9 seconds	11.7 seconds
0–60 mph	22.2 seconds	17.9 seconds
0–70 mph	33.3 seconds	28.8 seconds
	Top gear/3rd gear	Top gear (O/D)/3rd gear (O/D)
20–40 mph	12.1/8.5 seconds	9.3 (13.2)/5.9 (8.2) seconds
30–50 mph	12.8/9.2 seconds	9.7 (13.4)/7.1 (9.1) seconds
40–60 mph	14.8/12.2 seconds	12.4 (17.9)/10.4 (11.7) seconds
50–70 mph	17.3/– seconds	17.1 (27.1)/– (17.4) seconds
Fuel consumption	23.9 mpg (1594 miles)	20.8 mpg (1147 miles)

the Sceptre's original twin Zenith set up, and in October that year the all-synchromesh gearbox was fitted. Unlike the Hillman/Singer cars which now featured the squared up rear window treatment, the Sceptre was to remain unchanged in this respect throughout its production life. At this time (October 1964), the Singer Vogue acquired the high-output engine, thus putting its performance on to a similar level as that of the Humber but at the lower price of £844, although a further £52 had to be added if the overdrive was required on the cheaper car.

Both the Vogue and Sceptre received the five-bearing engine in September 1965, and with this engine again being in a higher state of tune than that of the Super Minx; 85 bhp at 5500 rpm now translated into a near 95 mph capability for the Singer and Humber variants. Recognition features unique to the Sceptre at this time were a different grille, and a pair of larger, $7^1/2$ inch diameter headlamps in the outer positions of its four-headlamp arrangements. In these configurations the models had become the Vogue Mk 4 and Sceptre Mk 2.

Like the Super Minx, the Vogue was replaced late in 1966 with an appropriate version of the new "Arrow" range, but the Sceptre continued for another year as the last of this line before the eventual appearance of a Sceptre version of the new series.

IMP MK1, MK2

Breaking away completely from the Rootes Group's traditional, and rather conservative approach to the building of motor cars, the Hillman Imp was not only something of a revolution in British small car design but was also being manufactured in a completely new factory, at Linwood in Scotland, specially built for the exclusive production of this new baby model and no other.

For this, their first attempt at a really small economical car, the Rootes engineers chose a rear-engined rear wheel drive layout, believing this to be a simpler solution to the space saving problems than a front-engine front wheel drive arrangement where the power has to be transmitted to the steerable wheels. Based loosely upon the 747 cc four-cylinder single overhead camshaft Coventry-Climax racing engine, the new Hillman Imp unit was an oversquare – 68 mm x 60.4 mm – design of 875 cc, and featured an aluminium cylinder block and cylinder head as on the Coventry-Climax product. The cylinders were siamezed in pairs, and separate cast-iron cylinder liners were used for the bores. The forged steel crankshaft was counterbalanced, and ran in three lead-indium main bearings. Chain driven, the single overhead camshaft operated valves which opened into wedge shaped combustion chambers; separate inlet and exhaust ports were used, and the compression ratio at 10:1 was very high by comparison with other British cars. A single Solex carburettor was used, and in an attempt to avoid accelerator linkage problems due to the rear-engine layout, a Dunlop pneumatic throttle control arrangement was adopted. This consisted of a cylinder below the accelerator pedal, in which there was a diaphragm that caused air to flow through plastic tubing to another cylinder; and completing the arrangement was a piston in this second cylinder operating a pushrod connected to the carburettor butterfly. Also taking account of the rear location was an automatic choke. 39 bhp at 5000 rpm, and 52 lbs/ft torque at 2800 rpm were good figures for an 875 cc engine, and promised a lively and economical performance.

A Laycock diaphragm-spring clutch was making its first appearance on a British production model, and in unit with the engine was an all indirect four-speed gearbox with integral final drive unit giving 15.2 mph/1000 rpm

Here's full-size family motoring with real performance, reliability and superb economy

-the amazing HILLMAN IMP

Despite its rear mounted engine, the Hillman Imp had the proportions and general appearance of a small conventional car. The Whitewall tyres were not standard equipment, but of course available at extra cost, and like many other manufacturers the Rootes Group often featured them in their advertisements and other promotional literature.

in top gear. Baulk-ring synchromesh was provided on all forward gears, and a short floor-mounted gearlever was employed. Aluminium was used again for the transmission casings, keeping the weight of the combined engine/gearbox package to little more than half of similarly sized conventional cast-iron assemblies. The whole unit was mounted very low down in the rear of the car, in a fore-and-aft arrangement with the engine being rearmost. Whereas the transmission part of the package was upright, the taller engine was canted over at 45 degrees as a further aid to a low centre of gravity, short drive shafts, with Metalastik bonded-rubber "Rotoflex" couplings inboard, transmitted the power to the independently suspended rear wheels.

Linked to the rear wheels thus, the gearbox was also attached at its forward end to the transverse member to which were also attached the semi-trailing arms of the independent rear suspension, and this whole sub-assembly could be quickly detached and wheeled away from the car if major attention was required. Coil springs and telescopic dampers completed the rear suspension. Despite the considerable use of aluminium in the power pack, approximately 60 per cent of the Imp's unladen weight was concentrated over the rear wheels, and to avoid the early tail-end breakaway and general instability encountered more often than not with rear-engined cars up to that time, great care was now taken in working out front suspension and steering geometry which would induce a stable understeering tendency. The set up actually chosen for the front end was a simple swing-axle arrangement, with the upright coil springs each embracing a telescopic damper. Rack and pinion steering gear was employed, and all of this, in conjunction with an understeer-inducing front 15 psi/rear 30 psi tyre pressure differential did in fact result in handling qualities which were to earn considerable praise; the tyres were 5.50 x 12 Dunlop C41s of lower profile than normal with crossplies. Able to cope sufficiently enough with the relatively lightweight (14 cwt) Imp's 80 mph performance was a Girling all drum braking system with 75 square inches of lining area.

The Imp's two-door bodyshell was an all steel monocoque structure, with suitable reinforcing at each end to take the mechanical sub-assemblies. Box section sills, and a small central tunnel which housed the gearchange linkage, brake lines etc., aided rigidity in the lower regions. Despite the rear location of the engine, the bodyshell was of three-box design, and with

This accessory advertisement also shows the short tail beneath which is housed the engine.

122

proportions which gave no outward suggestion of the unconventional nature of the mechanical layout. Although small in size, being only 11 feet 7 inches long and 5 feet 0$^{1}/4$ inch in width, the Imp nevertheless had a rather stylish appearance contributed to greatly by full length body fluting which gave a hint of a longer car than actually was the case.

Lifting up the rear lid revealed an engine compartment in which access to all items requiring regular attention was so good as to suggest that a considerable amount of thought had been given to the layout in this respect. There was of course no luggage space in this rear compartment, but a neat touch at this end of the car was that the rear window was hinged, and could be lifted tailgate-fashion for access to a rear shelf low down behind the rear seat; and furthermore, when unoccupied, the rear seat squab could be folded flat at the same level as the shelf, thus giving valuable extra luggage space whenever the Imp was being used in a two-seater role.

Access to a surprisingly roomy passenger compartment was good, the two 123

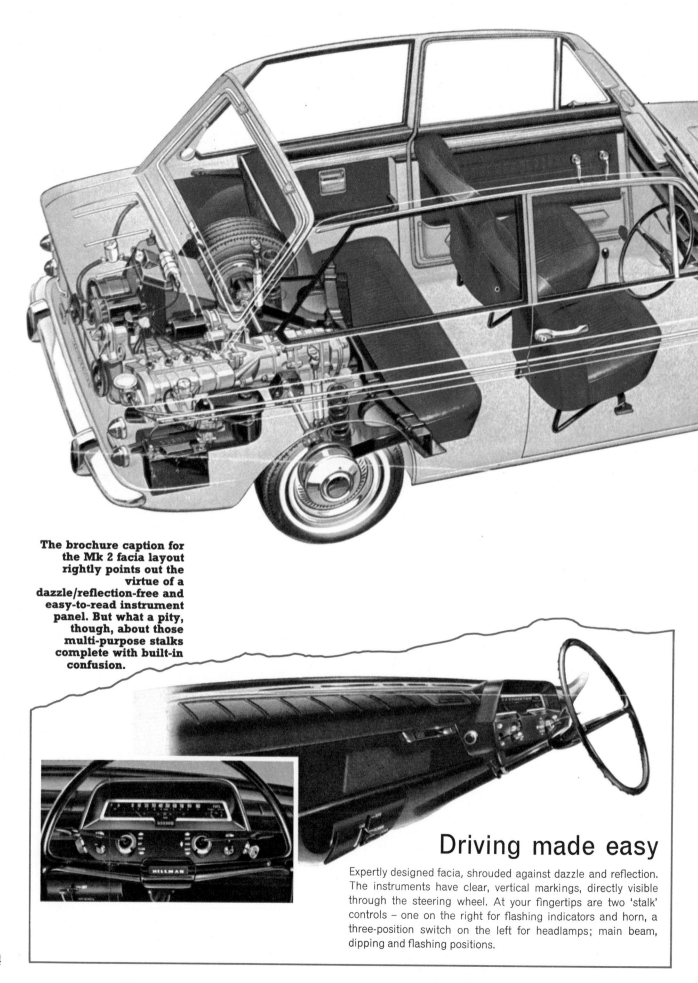

The brochure caption for the Mk 2 facia layout rightly points out the virtue of a dazzle/reflection-free and easy-to-read instrument panel. But what a pity, though, about those multi-purpose stalks complete with built-in confusion.

Driving made easy

Expertly designed facia, shrouded against dazzle and reflection. The instruments have clear, vertical markings, directly visible through the steering wheel. At your fingertips are two 'stalk' controls – one on the right for flashing indicators and horn, a three-position switch on the left for headlamps; main beam, dipping and flashing positions.

doors were wide enough to make rear seat entry quite easy past the tip-up front seats at each side. Vynide was used for the seating, and curved squabs on the individual front seats offered good sideways location. Wheelarch intrusion resulted in the footpedals being offset towards the middle, and a steering column angled slightly outwards towards the driver. Situated in a raised binnacle, an elongated speedometer was viewed through the upper half of a simple two-spoked steering wheel. A fuel gauge was the only other instrument fitted as standard, but an engine temperature gauge was an optional extra. A parcel shelf ran beneath the facia, with additional stowage for small items also being provided in the shape of open-top boxes situated on each door.

Rubber floor covering, and a generally very spartan trim level was to be seen on the standard model being offered, but at only a small extra charge was a De Luxe car which was to come very well equipped by the small-car standards of the time. This featured a fully carpeted floor, twin sunvisors, screenwasher, and the heating and demisting system amongst its standard equipment. Fresh air for the heating arrangements was drawn in through a small grille under the front bumper and directed to the heater matrix mounted underneath the facia. Linking this to the engine's cooling system radiator at the rear were hoses running through the body sills to the engine compartment.

At the front a full width lid opened to reveal a small luggage compartment, the front portion of which was taken up by the spare wheel situated in an upright position immediately behind the body front panel. Also taking up considerable space here was the flat 7 gallon fuel tank immediately behind the spare wheel, and which reduced the depth of the compartment to just 11 inches. The spare wheel, and a bumper bar far too small to be effective in anything other than a very minor shunt, offered only meagre protection for the front-mounted fuel tank which could be seen as a major drawback of this rear-engined layout.

Announced in May 1963, at £508 for the standard model, and £532 for the much better equipped De Luxe saloon, the Imp was undercut in the price lists by the BMC Mini (£448 & £493) at whose market it appeared to be aimed. By comparison the Imp looked much more like a full-size car, and

A brochure illustration of the Mk 2 model showing the unconventional mechanical layout of the Imp. The four-seat roominess is well-apparent here, as are the usefully-sized bins in the door and rear side panel. The fuel filler and hydraulic reservoir are accessible just beneath the front compartment lid.

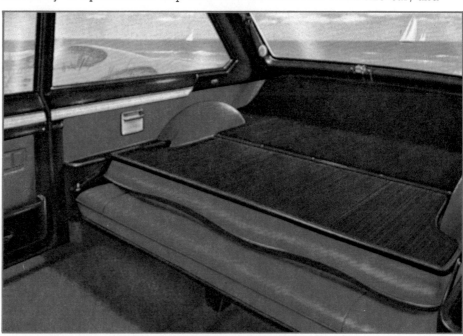

An estate car-like rear end arrangement gave the Imp greater versatility than some other small saloons, and the model's large window area gives a nice impression of spaciousness.

A Mk 2 emblem identifies the post October 1965 Imp equipped with an improved cylinder head.

Just as seen here, the Chamois always came equipped with overriders and wheeltrims, and was badged as a Singer product as can just be detected here under the numberplate.

The rather sporty-looking Imp Californian was a derivative which revived a name from Hillman's past, "Californian" having been the title bestowed upon a two-door fixed-head coupe Hillman Minx in the early 1950s.

was offering the greater amount of internal room that its larger outside dimensions suggested, although it was still definitely only a four-seat car. In many ways it was just as technically innovative as the BMC baby, and on the road, with its maximum speed of 80 mph and a 23 second 0–60 mph capability, it would comfortably outrun the Mini, and at cruising speeds in the 50 to 60 mph range it was also the more economical of the two, being capable of returning a remarkable 50 mpg at a constant 50 mph. Purely pricewise, and discounting the venerable Morris Minor, the Imp's closest modern rival was the Ford Anglia 105E, at £514 and £538 in its standard and De Luxe variants. Here again the Imp was both quicker and more economical, whilst offering virtually identical interior dimensions in which to comfortably accommodate four persons. From all of this it appeared that the Rootes Group had a winner on their hands, and there were indeed forecasts of quite tremendous sales. In the event, however, the Imp proved unable to make a significant impact, achieving only a modest sales success by comparison with the BMC and Ford market leaders at this end of the scale. Perhaps contributing to this situation were a number of early reliability problems, although these should have really been no surprise considering the complex nature of the Imp by comparison with the usually so conventional Hillman cars. Some problems were solved fairly quickly, such as replacing the troublesome automatic choke with a manual control, but the Imp still failed to capture the imagination of the buying public in anything like the way the BMC front-wheel-drive cars had done.

October 1964 saw the introduction of a better-trimmed version, badged as a Singer Chamois, but destined to be referred to as the Singer Imp by most people. Bumper overriders, a dummy front grille, chrome side strips and drip rail capping, and the introduction of rubbing strips on the engine compartment top were recognition features. Bright metal wheeltrim discs were standard, and the keen-eyed observer would perhaps spot that the Singer's wheels were wider than those of the Hillman version, and were shod with radial-ply tyres.

The tyres apart, the technical specification was exactly as the Imp, but in respect of interior appointments the Chamois was altogether more lavish. A higher quality PVC was used for the trim, whilst lower front seats gave

127

another inch or so of headroom, and featured squabs of greater curvature giving even better location than those in the Imp. Gauges for engine temperature and oil pressure were included as standard, and a padded facia top was now to be seen running above a new wood veneer facia board. A similar treatment to the facia continued along the sides of the car interior immediately below window level, whilst adding considerably to the refinement when running was the application of much sound-deadening material between the engine and passenger compartments. These improvements added up to a still very reasonable price of £582, at which this Singer-badged variant would seem to have been better value than the cheaper, but rather plainer Hillmans. Indeed, the success of the better-equipped versions resulted in the deletion of the standard Imp in September 1965, at which time the model went into Mk 2 form with the range now comprising the Imp De Luxe, Super Imp, and Singer Chamois.

The Super Imp, at £566, came nicely between the Imp De Luxe and the Chamois which were now at £539 and £590. The wheel-discs, its own dummy grille, side strips and "Super Imp" badges identified the mid-range model which also had a rather better interior than the De Luxe Imp, although without the polished woodwork of the Chamois. Additional sound-deadening material, improved trim levels, and the application of underseal had resulted in the Imps putting on weight, and although no power increase was being quoted, the Mk 2 models did feature a new cylinder head with bigger valves, and a larger carburettor. Even so, the Mk 2 cars proved to be not quite so quick as the earlier models.

And again, another name from a previous Minx now applied to the Imp when in the form of a Hillman Husky estate car. LRD 368F is pictured recently amongst other surviving Imps at an old-car gathering.

The new cylinder head was a stiffer casting than previously, in an attempt to lessen the incidence of warped cylinder heads and blown cylinder head gaskets occuring when Imp engines overheated. A further attempt at lessening this problem came late in 1966 when the cylinder block casting was also made stiffer, and now featured revised threaded holes for the cylinder head bolts. The overheating problems were in part due to the aluminium engine corroding internally and producing a powdery substance which would silt up the radiator tubes and also wear out the water pump. Meticulous cooling system maintenance, such as very regular flushing out, and all year round use of an anti-freeze solution with corrosion inhibitors specifically recommended for aluminium engines would however largely overcome the problem. In other respects the Imp engine was a durable unit which could withstand habitual hard usage very well, and cope with greater power outputs than the standard production model. For competition purposes Rootes themselves produced a short production run "homologation special" in 1966. Known as the Rallye Imp, this featured a larger bore diameter which increased the capacity to 998 cc, and with twin Stromberg carburettors this engine produced 65 bhp at 6200 rpm which was sufficient to propel the Hillman at speeds in excess of 90 mph.

Datapanel: Hillman Imp, Imp Mk 2

Engine	4 cyl, sohc	
Capacity	875 cc	
Bore	68 mm	
Stroke	60.4 mm	
Compression ratio	10.0:1	
Max BHP	39 nett @ 5000 rpm	
Max torque	52 lbs/ft @ 2800 rpm	
Gearing	15.2 mph/1000 rpm	
Tyres	5.50 x 12	
Kerb weight	14 cwt (14$\frac{1}{2}$ cwt Mk 2)	
Overall length	11 ft 7 in	
Overall width	5 ft 0$\frac{1}{4}$ in	
Wheelbase	6 ft 10 in	
Performance		
	"Autocar" 3rd May 1963	"Motor" R/T No. 9/66 Imp Mk 2
Max speed		
Top gear	80.8 mph (mean) 83.0 mph (best)	75.5 mph (mean) 79.7 mph (best)
3rd gear	71 mph	64 mph
2nd gear	46 mph	41 mph
1st gear	25 mph	22 mph
Acceleration		
0–30 mph	5.4 seconds	5.7 seconds
0–50 mph	14.7 seconds	16.0 seconds
0–60 mph	23.7 seconds	25.5 seconds
0–70 mph	38.4 seconds	48.9 seconds
	Top gear/3rd gear	Top gear/3rd gear
20–40 mph	14.2/8.6 seconds	13.9/8.6 seconds
30–50 mph	14.1/9.9 seconds	15.9/10.5 seconds
40–60 mph	19.3/14.6 seconds	19.0/15.4 seconds
50–70 mph	23.0/– seconds	38.6/– seconds
Fuel consumption	38.1 mpg (2120 miles)	31.3 mpg (1467 miles)

Following this, in October 1966 regular production models with higher output 875 cc engines were added to the range; these also used twin Stromberg carburettors, and developed 51 bhp at 6100 rpm. Yet another new cylinder head with further enlarged inlet valves, a re-profiled camshaft, stronger pistons, and an oil cooler were other features of this uprated engine which was to be found in Imps badged as either a Singer Chamois Sport, or a Sunbeam Imp Sport. In view of a near 90 mph capability, harder brake linings and a vacuum-servo were fitted, whilst inside these cars was rather more comprehensive instrumentation, and lower front seats with reclining squabs. At £665 irrespective of which badge was being displayed, these go-faster Imps were not quite a match in sheer performance terms for the BMC Mini Cooper (£600), but were offering an altogether higher trim level which to some people would justify the extra cost by comparison.

The ordinary Hillman Imp De Luxe and Super Imp models were continuing at prices of £549 and £576, at which they were not only now being undercut by BMC's Mini, but by the Ford Anglia as well. Nevertheless, the model continued to sell steadily, and in fact was to remain in production well into the 1970s under a variety of permutations behind Hillman, Singer, and Sunbeam badges.

In sharp contrast to the company's new Imp range, the Hillman Minx continued as an utterly conventional model. This late-1963 advertisement announces the Series V of this well-proven line which stretched back to 1956.

MINX SERIES V, VI

The success of the Super Minx had not apparently been at the expense of the well-established smaller Minx model. This had gone into Series 111C configuration upon acquiring the 1592 cc engine in August 1961 just prior to the release of the Super Minx, and was redesignated simply Minx 1600 early in 1962. With a buoyant market for this slightly smaller type of car remaining, a major rework of the Minx was now undertaken in order to ensure its competitiveness for a considerable further spell, with the result of this appearing in September 1963 as the Hillman Minx Series V.

Based on the Series 1/11/111 bodyshell, and utilising the same sturdy underbody with its front and rear longitudinal stiffeners finishing where they met the transverse stiffening members which linked up with the inner sills, the Series V body differed quite considerably in respect of outward appearance. At the front, a lower bonnet line was introduced to give better visibility; as before, the new bonnet top was also counterbalanced, and beneath this was a new and much simpler full width grille of horizontal bars. The previous outwardly-curved fins which had characterized the model at the rear from Series 111A onwards were now deleted, leaving a rather plain rear wing line. Gone too was the very characteristic wrap-around rear window which had been a feature of this bodyshell since its first appearance in 1956. With the new rear screen came new rear quarter panels, and new wider rear doors to suit; fixed quarter windows were included in these doors. The roof line was slightly lower now, and also affecting the appearance were 13 inch diameter roadwheels which looked rather too small in the wheelarches designed to give sufficient clearance for the 15 inch wheels of the previous Minx. A useful improvement not readily apparent was an increase in capacity from $7^1/4$ to 10 gallons for the fuel tank residing beneath the boot floor.

Only a very thin chrome strip broke the expanse of the body sides, although a much better-looking double strip outlining a narrow band of different colour was included if the optional two-tone paint scheme was specified, and with which the alternative colour also appeared on the roof.

Bearing a 1964 registration, a fine-looking example is seen here pictured recently amongst some other collectible Rootes models.

The plain bumper bars were without overriders, but additional bright metal
was to be seen around the screens as well as the usual door handles,
hubcaps etc., and the overall effect was neat.

The interior had been substantially redesigned, with a great improvement
to be seen in the new facia in which the instrumentation was now
immediately in front of the driver rather than in the centre of the facia as
before. Two large dials flanked the steering column, with that on the left
being the speedometer, whilst the other one housing the fuel gauge also
featured two vacant spaces in which the optional ammeter and an engine
temperature gauge could be fitted. A small blank dial between the two large
ones was for the optional oil pressure gauge, whilst in the centre of the
facia now was a similar space for an electric clock. A glove box faced the
passenger, and there was useful further stowage space on a full width shelf
below the facia. The front edge of the shelf was padded, as was the facia
top. The flat steering wheel had a full circle hornring, and the front doors
had the benefit of swivelling quarter windows; twin sunvisors were fitted
too, but in other respects the interior was rather plain.

There were no armrests to be seen; the door trims were without any
pattern, and a rubber matting covered the floor. PVC seat coverings were
of a simple pleated design. Individual front seats replaced the previous
Minx's bench seat, and were similar in construction to those of the Super

Minx, having foam cushions over a rubber diaphragm. Lower than the previous front bench seat, they provided approximately 2 inches more headroom than before. An increase in the range of front seat adjustment from the rather meagre 3 inches of the earlier car, to 5 inches now, improved the situation for taller drivers whilst still leaving a minimum 6 inches rear compartment knee-room.

The 1592 cc engine was remaining in exactly the same state of tune as on the superseded Minx 111C, with 52.8 bhp at 4100 rpm, and 86.8 lbs/ft torque at 2200 rpm. Still without synchromesh on first gear, the four-speed gearbox with floor mounted lever also remained as before, but the axle ratio was raised to 3.89:1 in order to compensate for the smaller wheels and tyres. This axle, and the wheels, were as on the current Super Minx (Mk 2), and gave overall gearing of 17.2 mph/1000 rpm. An optional transmission was the Borg Warner Model 35 automatic, replacing the Smiths "Easidrive" automatic gearbox which had been seen on the earlier Minx models. With the automatic option now came the more powerful (58 bhp @ 4400 rpm) version of the 1592 cc engine as used in the Super Minx, and as a result of the slight increase in power the Series V Minx automatic proved to be one of the very few cars on which the performance suffered very little if at all by comparison with its manual gearbox counterpart.

At the front, the coil spring and wishbone independent suspension was as before apart from slightly softer springs. The rear longitudinal leaf springs were also slightly softer, and revised damper settings were introduced at this end of the car, with these changes in total resulting in a more softer riding Minx than hitherto. Recirculating ball steering gear was retained, albeit slightly lower geared now, but a big change was to be seen in the provision of front disc brakes. These were exactly as on the Mk 2 Super

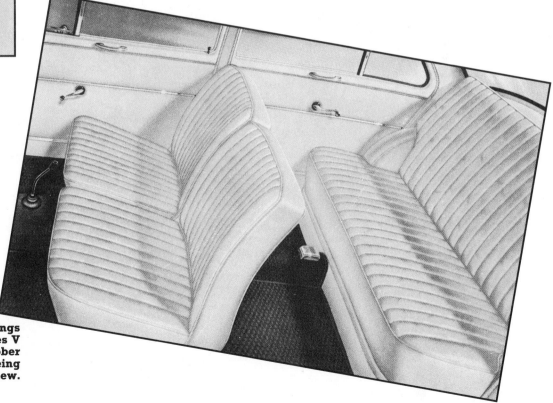

Simple furnishings characterized the Series V Minx, with the rubber floor covering being evident in this view.

Meet the wonderful new Singer Gazelle. See the clean, new styling . . . the sleek, low roofline . . . the luxury and space inside. Note the improvements! Powerful front disc brakes. No greasing points—low servicing costs. Lighter, more positive steering and self-adjusting clutch. Improved ride comfort and road holding. Luxurious individual front seats, separately adjustable. More legroom in the rear compartment and easier access through wider opening rear doors. Improved visibility. Handsome walnut facia with instruments placed before the driver. Full width safety pad. Heater fitted as standard equipment.

Handy front and rear parcel trays. Lockable glove box. Screenwashers. Overriders. And a truly magnificent finish—with a wide choice of attractive single and duo-tone colour schemes. That's the new Gazelle. And that's value. Ask for a demonstration ride today.

£598 plus p.t. £125-2-11

OPTIONAL EXTRAS: BORG-WARNER AUTOMATIC TRANSMISSION OR OVERDRIVE ON 3RD AND 4TH GEARS. WHITEWALL TYRES.

SINGER GAZELLE

A striking advertisement for the new Singer Gazelle which, with more opulant appointments and its higher standard equipment level seemed worth the extra cost for those who could afford it.

Minx, and were in conjunction with the existing 9 inch diameter drums at the rear.

Whereas previous editions of the Minx had included standard and De Luxe models, with the standard version sometimes listed as the Minx Special, the Series V was to be available as just one model, priced at £645. Although extra was charged for the heater (£18/17s/6d) and windscreen washers (£1/15s/0d), the Series V Minx was a good-value-for-money car at this price. By comparison, a Cortina Super 1500 was listed at £688.

A badge-engineered Singer Gazelle derivative had appeared alongside the earlier models in this long-running Minx series, originally with its own Singer overhead camshaft engine, but later with the same power unit as the cheaper Hillmans. These Singers had generally been considered much more upmarket than the Hillman, but the lack of a De Luxe Minx in the new Series V guise resulted in the Gazelle Series V, which appeared one week after the Minx, now being regarded more as just a De Luxe Minx than had previously been the case.

Once again sharing the same bodyshell, and identical mechanical specification, the Gazelle was recognisable by the neat upright Singer grille incorporated into the bonnet top at the front, and the square rather than horizontal rear numberplate situated on the boot lid. A broader "flash" along the sides, and in which a second colour could be specified at no extra cost, bumper overriders, and wheeltrims were other standard Gazelle features. Although the supplementary instruments were still only optional extras, the heater and windscreen washers were standard equipment on the Gazelle, and the seating and door trims were in a higher grade PVC than on the Minx. Of exactly the same layout, the facia was finished in walnut veneer, and this was to be seen also on the door cappings. Armrests were still a surprising omission, but carpeting did now cover the rear compartment floor and appeared also on the front transmission tunnel, leaving rubber mats now just for the front footwells.

In all, at £723, the Gazelle seemed perhaps even better value than the Hillman when taking into account the appreciably more comprehensive trim and equipment level. In addition to the automatic transmission option as on the Hillman, Gazelle buyers were offered the further option of a Laycock

Another brochure illustration depicts the neat facia layout including all the optional instrumentation, heater, and radio. The motif representing the three Coventry Spires provides for an elegant steering wheel hub.

Both Minx and Gazelle became Series VI late in 1965 upon the adoption of the 1725 cc engine. At this time also a production economy could be seen with the Gazelle also receiving the Minx bonnet and sidelamp units; it did however retain a Singer-style grille, albeit in much reduced form. A 1966 example, MGT 291D, seen here in 1985, is looking good as it approaches its 20th birthday.

135

Datapanel: Hillman Minx/Singer Gazelle Series V, VI

	Series V	Series VI
Engine	4 cyl, ohv	4 cyl, ohv
Capacity	1592 cc	1725 cc
Bore	81.5 mm	81.5 mm
Stroke	76.2 mm	82.5 mm
Compression ratio	8.3:1	8.4:1
Max BHP	52.8 nett @ 4100 rpm	58.5 nett @ 4200 rpm
Max torque	86.8 lbs/ft @ 2100 rpm	92.2 lbs/ft @ 2200 rpm
Gearing	17.2 mph/1000 rpm	17.2 mph/1000 rpm
	16.2 mph/1000 rpm (4.22:1 axle)	16.2 mph/1000 rpm (4.22:1 axle)
Tyres	6.00 x 13	6.00 x 13
Kerb weight	19^1/$_2$ cwt	19^1/$_2$ cwt
Overall length	13 ft 7^1/$_2$ in	13 ft 7^1/$_2$ in
Overall width	5 ft 0^1/$_2$ in	5 ft 0^1/$_2$ in
Wheelbase	8 ft	8 ft
Performance		
	"The Motor" RT No. 42/63	"Motor" RT No. 20/66 (Singer Gazelle with overdrive & 4.22:1 axle)
Max speed		
Top gear	77.2 mph (mean)	81.3 mph (mean)
	82.0 mph (best)	87.4 mph (best)
3rd gear	71 mph	63 mph
2nd gear	47 mph	41 mph
1st gear	26 mph	26 mph
Acceleration		
0–30 mph	6.2 seconds	5.6 seconds
0–50 mph	15.8 seconds	13.5 seconds
0–60 mph	26.2 seconds	19.5 seconds
0–70 mph	45.9 seconds	31.7 seconds
	Top gear/3rd gear	Top gear (O/D) 3rd gear (O/D)
20–40 mph	12.2/8.7 seconds	9.7 (14.2/7.0 (8.5) seconds
30–50 mph	14.2/10.3 seconds	10.6 (15.0)/8.2 (9.7) seconds
40–60 mph	19.0/15.6 seconds	13.1 (18.0)/11.1 (11.9) seconds
50–70 mph	31.2/– seconds	18.7 (27.4)/– (18.6) seconds
Fuel consumption	26.8 mpg (1138 miles)	24.1 mpg (2200 miles)

overdrive to supplement the manual gearbox. This cost £51, and Gazelles so equipped came with a lower axle ratio of 4.22:1. This gave 16.2 mph/1000 rpm on direct top gear, with 20.2 mph/1000 rpm in overdrive. With the availability also of a steering column gearchange, it was possible to tailor the Gazelle's transmission arrangements even more closely to individual tastes.

Weighing in as they did at over 19 cwt, these Series V models were not particularly fast cars by 1.6 litre standards, with barely 80 mph available flat out and requiring 26 seconds or so to reach 60 mph from rest. But, the real appeal of these cars lay in their combination of solid build, tasteful trim and appearance, and well-proven dependability, all of which made a lot of sound common sense to many people who were pleased to see this popular Rootes theme continuing in production.

Both cars received a diaphragm-spring clutch and all-synchromesh gearbox in September 1964, at which time reclining front seat squabs were introduced, and the screenwashers standardized on the Minx. In September 1965 the Minx and Gazelle became the Series VI models when the five-main-bearing 1725 cc engine was adopted. In this application the unit developed 58.5 bhp at 4200 rpm coupled with a really useful 92.2 lbs/ft of torque still at only 2200 rpm. This was sufficient to put the model into the genuine 80 mph category along with worthwhile gains in acceleration throughout the range, whilst fuel economy remained in the 25 to 35 mpg bracket much as before.

The Singer now featured the Hillman bonnet, but beneath which there remained a cut-down version of the Singer radiator grille set into the Minx-style front panel, and now flanked by the Minx-type sidelamp units.

Bearing in mind the greater performance, and the improvement in mechanical refinement imparted by the five-bearing engine, at £660 for the Minx and £757 for the Gazelle, the Series VI models seemed to be offering better value than at any other time for this line which could now be traced back almost ten years. This was however, the last stage of their development, and late in 1966 they were phased out to make way for new models bearing the same names, but based on the new Rootes "Arrow" range of cars of which the Hillman Hunter had been the first to appear.

4

STANDARD-TRIUMPH

TRIUMPH HERALD, HERALD S, HERALD 1200, HERALD 12/50

Apart from inheriting the excellent little 948 cc engine of its immediate predecessors, the Standard Ten "Gold Star", and Pennant models, the Standard-Triumph company's new Triumph Herald differed greatly in almost every other respect. For several reasons, not least of which was a difficulty now in being able to obtain completed bodyshells from outside sources as had been the case with the preceding Standard Eight and Ten bodies, a reversion to the separate body and chassis method of car construction had taken place for the new model. This, and all-independent suspension, were sufficient to set the Triumph Herald well-apart from other small British saloons upon its announcement in April 1959.

The chassis was of the backbone type, with the two full-length box-section longitudinal members running very close to each other under the middle portion of the car, where they were tied together at three closely-spaced points, before splaying outwards. From both sides of this backbone, three outriggers, one at each end of the passenger area plus a central one, extended to almost full car width, and were linked together at their outer ends by further longitudinal members, thus completing a well-braced full framework under the passenger cabin. Ahead of this the two main longitudinal members re-assumed a parallel course to the front of the car where they were angled upwards ahead of the front suspension pick-up points, whilst at the rear these same members continued their outward and again now slightly upwards run to terminate at the extreme rear corners of the car.

Separately bolted-on attachments to the chassis rails carried the independent front suspension units, each of which comprised upper and lower unequal length wishbones, and an inward-angled coil spring embracing a hydraulic telescopic damper; a forward-mounted anti-roll bar linked the lower wishbone. Rack-and-pinion steering gear was used, with the rack being the centre member of a three-piece track-rod arrangement mounted ahead of the axle line. The steering column was adjustable for length, with a good feature being that the adjustment would "give" above a force of approximately 2g, so allowing the column to telescope downwards should the driver be thrown forward onto it in an accident.

At the rear was a simple swing-axle independent rear suspension system, with each of the open axle drive shafts being universally-jointed to the fixed height drive unit. A single leaf-spring was mounted transversely above the axle, with its central attachment point being an integral part of the final

Both a saloon and sporting fixed-head coupe were available upon the Herald's introduction.

drive housing; at its extremities, this spring was located at the upper end of extensions to the hub assemblies. Fore-and-aft location was by radius rods running forward from the lower part of these hub extensions to the rearmost chassis outrigger. Immediately aft of the axle line, inclined slightly inwards were telescopic dampers attached at their base to the hub extensions and at their upper end to upswept brackets from the chassis frame.

The all-drum Girling hydraulic braking system comprised 8 inch diameter drums at the front, and 7 inch diameter at the rear, with a total lining area of 73 square inches. A 5.20 x 13 tyre and rim combination completed the running gear.

As already mentioned, the 948 cc engine, with bore and stroke measurements of 63 mm x 76 mm, respectively, was that of the preceding Standard Ten. This featured a deep-skirt cylinder block in which the bores were siamezed in pairs, and a counterbalanced crankshaft running in three main bearings. With a single Solex carburettor, and a compression ratio of 8.0:1, this engine produced 34.5 bhp at 4500 rpm, with 48 lbs/ft torque being developed at 2750 rpm. The four-speed gearbox had synchromesh between the upper three ratios, with gear selection by a short remote control floor

A lovely period publicity photograph shows off to perfection the Herald's smart profile.

mounted lever which proved to be extremely accurate in operation. A rear axle ratio of 4.875:1 gave low overall gearing of just 13.3 mph/1000 rpm, and was chosen to allow for the increase in weight now to 16 cwt unladen that compared rather unfavourably with the 14¹/₂ cwt of the Standard Ten, and which had pulled a slightly higher gear.

As the Herald was to go into production in two variants, with these being a normal two-door four-seater passenger saloon, and a two-seater sporting Fixed-Head Coupe, (albeit with two "occasional" rear seats) there was a revised mechanical specification for the latter in order to provide it with greater performance. With a raised compression ratio of 8.5:1, a high-lift camshaft, and twin SU carburettors, the power output of the Coupe engine was increased to 45 bhp at 5500 rpm, whilst an axle ratio of 4.55:1 in this case raised the overall gearing to 14.2 mph/1000 rpm.

No less interesting than the mechanical specification and unusual chassis details was the all-steel bodywork of which the whole was made up of several large welded-up sub-assemblies which were then bolted to each other and to the chassis frame. The main bulkhead/scuttle assembly also included the windscreen surround and approximately half of the passenger compartment floor. The remainder of the floor was included in another major assembly which also consisted of the heelboard, wheelarches, and rear wings. The two passenger doors, and the bootlid were the same for both saloon and Coupe models, with the differences being confined to the separately fitted roof sections. Of the latter, that for the saloon was notable for its extremely thin pillars which gave excellent all-round visibility, whereas the shorter roof of the Coupe included unglazed rear quarter panels.

Doors of 40 inch width, and tip-up front seats gave good access to both front and rear of a passenger compartment that was particularly light and airy thanks to the very large window area. In addition to the normal fore-and-aft adjustment the fixed-back seats could also be set at any of four different angles. This facility, in conjunction with the adjustable steering column was such as to ensure that almost all drivers, whatever their stature, could find an ideal driving position in the Herald. The seat and side trim material was PVC, whilst carpeting covered the floor, and there were such items as the heater, passenger's sunvisor with vanity mirror, windscreen washers, wind-down windows and swivelling front quarter windows all included in the standard specification. Instrumentation however was minimal, with just one dial incorporating the speedometer and a fuel gauge being set into a plain facia panel. The speedometer was viewed through the upper half of a steering wheel which was of an attractively-styled two-spoke design. Mounted centrally on the facia was the switchgear, and a cubby hole without a lid faced the passenger. A parcel net was situated below the facia, and the transmission tunnel included a small oddments tray.

Opening from floor level, the boot lid was self-supporting by means of a ratchet type strut, and revealed a conveniently shaped compartment in which the floor sloped gently forward at the angle dictated by the upswept rear chassis members. There was no rear passenger compartment bulkhead, and the rear seat squab was therefore arranged so that it could be folded flat in estate car fashion so allowing the occasional transport of longer loads if required. The 7 gallon fuel tank was mounted in an upright position in the nearside wing, and encroaching slightly upon the boot space, but the spare wheel housed in a well, and concealed by a circular cover, left an unobstructed floor.

At the front of the car there was a lower apron running full width, and a fixed grille above this. These fixtures were entirely separate from the rest of the bodywork, which included here a one-piece bonnet and front wings assembly which was pivoted at its front corners, and secured to the scuttle/bulkhead sides by catches at its other end. With these catches released, the whole assembly could be tipped forward, thus giving unrivalled underbonnet accessibility for both routine service and major mechanical work.

In all, therefore, the Triumph Herald was an eminently practical small car, but in which practicality had nevertheless not been bought at the expense of style. On the contrary, in fact, as within the modest overall length and width of 12 feet 9 inches, and 5 feet, the Herald was of a crisp and smart appearance which did credit to Italian stylist Giovanni Michelotti who, in conjunction with coachbuilders Vignale of Turin, had produced the Herald prototype bodies for Standard-Triumph.

With just one trim and equipment level, there being no ''basic'' or De Luxe variations, the Herald was priced at £702 upon its introduction in April 1959, and at which it was not a cheap car for its type, being opposed as it was by such as the Austin A40 De Luxe at £650, and the Morris Minor two-door De Luxe at £618.

With a little over 70 mph available, and able to reach 60 mph from rest in

Happy days – in a Triumph Herald convertible. The separate chassis frame made production of a Herald convertible a relatively simple matter, with the result being a price penalty of only 9% by comparison with the saloon.

Raising the hood was said to take only two minutes, and when in this position the top was of neat appearance. The large bonnet ornament is of course the handle necessary for raising the car's entire front section when the lower catches (seen just aft of the wheelarch) are released.

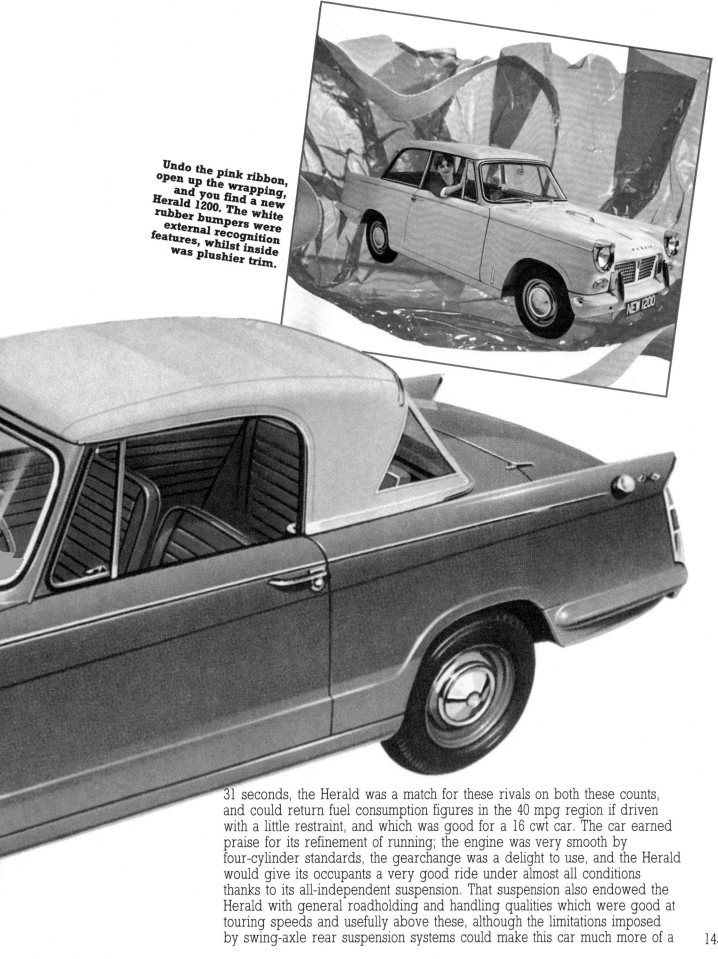

Undo the pink ribbon, open up the wrapping, and you find a new Herald 1200. The white rubber bumpers were external recognition features, whilst inside was plushier trim.

31 seconds, the Herald was a match for these rivals on both these counts, and could return fuel consumption figures in the 40 mpg region if driven with a little restraint, and which was good for a 16 cwt car. The car earned praise for its refinement of running; the engine was very smooth by four-cylinder standards, the gearchange was a delight to use, and the Herald would give its occupants a very good ride under almost all conditions thanks to its all-independent suspension. That suspension also endowed the Herald with general roadholding and handling qualities which were good at touring speeds and usefully above these, although the limitations imposed by swing-axle rear suspension systems could make this car much more of a

143

The new, new, Herald model 'S'

S for saving The new Herald S saves you pounds, without losing any of the Herald mechanical marvels.
S for special The new Herald S is special in 7 ways. Here they are. Seven good reasons why the new Herald S is the finest value on four wheels.

1 Independent suspension on all wheels
2 Garage maintenance once in 3,000 miles
3 Turns in 25 feet, easiest car to park
4 Double-backbone steel-girder chassis
5 93% all-round view for safer driving
6 72 different driving-seat positions
7 So safe that you can get lower insurance

With the advent of the 1200 models, only a cut-price Herald 'S' continued with the 948 cc engine, and could be identified by the plain mesh grille. The lack of a bonnet handle may also be noted, and was a state of affairs which soon after spread throughout the range.

''handful'' than conventionally-suspended models when being pressed very hard through corners.

If the Herald was good on the open road, it was none the less so in town, where its remarkable 25 ft turning circle would often give it quite considerable advantage over others in tightly restricted situations, and this feature alone would endear it to many over the ensuing years.

The Coupe's twin carburettor engine became an option on the Herald saloons later in 1959, for an extra £35, and with this the saloon moved into the 75 mph category. Broadening the appeal further, in March 1960 came the announcement of the Herald convertible, at £766, with manually operated hood which was of the simple two-position type with no half-way De Ville position. A large window area, including separate quarter windows was an excellent feature of this hood when in its raised position. Complete concealment when lowered was another good point, and in this configuration the Herald convertible was very neat indeed; hood stowage however did encroach on passenger space, and the convertible Herald's rear seat was consequently much smaller and narrower than the saloon's.

An economy Herald ''S'' model was introduced early in 1961, with cheapened trim, devoid of a heater, and generally less well equipped, but selling at a price of £648 which was a worthwhile reduction from the £702 of the fully equipped regular Herald models. The S model in fact soon became the only 948 cc engined car in the line up, as in April 1961 the Herald 1200 appeared, after which the other smaller-engined models, including the twin carburettor cars, were phased out.

The principle feature of the 1200 was the enlarged capacity engine which was actually of 1147 cc. This had been achieved by enlarging the bore size to 69.3 mm, and had necessitated what was almost wholly a new cylinder block, with each pair of siamezed bores now being offset from the centre line. The stroke remained at 76 mm, although the crankshaft was new and all the bearings were now of lead-indium. An improved oil pump was fitted and a full-flow oil filter replaced the previous by-pass type. Still with a compression ratio of 8.0:1, and retaining a single Solex carburettor, the 1147

When it appeared in May 1962 there was no mistaking the six-cylinder-engined Vitesse when viewed head-on, but in other respects it had all the appearance of a Herald.

TRIUMPH VITESSE
New 6-cylinder magic

THE SMOOTH SIX 6-cylinder energy in a 17-cwt car! That's the Triumph Vitesse, the only car of its class in the world to have a 6-cylinder engine. The brand-new 1596 cc engine gives you a top speed of over 90 mph. And you sprint through the gears from 0 to 60 in 17.1 seconds.

THE SUPPLE SIX The Vitesse has all the mechanical magic of the Herald. Independent suspension front and back, and the Herald turning circle of only 25 ft.

THE SMART SIX Vitesse beauty is in the *concours d'elegance* class. And she's smart under the surface, too.

Clever design virtually eliminates grease points to cut servicing down to just once in 3,000 miles.

THE SAFE SIX 4-eye vision at night, sturdy steel chassis, front-wheel disc brakes. Take out a new Triumph Vitesse, and recapture the joy of driving a car designed to make motoring the pleasure it should be. Any Standard-Triumph dealer will be pleased to arrange it for you. You'll be under no pressure to buy, but be warned. The Vitesse is a temptress.

Vitesse saloon £837.0.3 *inc. p.t.*   Vitesse convertible £893.7.9 *inc. p.t.*
Duotone paintwork £9.12.6 extra

STANDARD TRIUMPH
A member of the Leyland Motors Group

145

cc unit developed 39 nett bhp at the same 4500 rpm, with a much greater
percentage increase in maximum torque which was up by no less than 12
lbs/ft, to a nett figure now of 60 lbs/ft at just 2250 rpm.

White rubber bumpers, the word "Herald" now rather than "Triumph" on
the bonnet, and a "1200" script on the boot were external identification
features now, whilst inside there was a wood veneer facia, complete with a
lockable glove box lid, which gave a more expensive look to this latest
Herald. Sprung seat squabs rather than the previous webbing and padding
were claimed to be an improvement; but a disappointment was that the rear
seat squab was now fixed, and so the Herald saloon lost some of its useful
emergency load carrying capacity. A price increase of only £6 accompanied
these changes with the saloon, coupe, and convertible now being listed at
£708, £736, and £772, respectively, and all cars now having identical engines
with no twin carburettor option. A performance boost which included a 75
mph-plus maximum, and a standstill to 60 mph capability now of around 24
seconds, also included much-improved flexibility, and had been achieved
with only very little adverse effect on fuel consumption as the 1200 models
were equipped with a 4.11:1 axle which raised the overall gearing.

Extending the line up to five models came the Herald 1200 estate car just
one month later, at £799, and featuring quite considerable strengthening by
comparison with the other Heralds. Boxed-in cant rails and rear pillars, and
thicker sheet steel for the extended roof combined to give good rigidity,
whilst down below, the estate car chassis differed from that of the saloon by
including boxed-in rear members. A 9 gallon fuel tank replaced the other
Heralds' 7 gallon tank, and a stiffer rear spring, revised damper settings
and slightly larger, 5.60 x 13 tyres were other changes with which to cope
effectively with increased loads. Spring-loaded struts supported the large
lift-up tailgate, and with the rear seat squabs folded forward loads of up to 5
feet 4 inches in length could be accommodated.

Whereas distinctly sporting editions of most small and medium family saloons gained their extra performance from highly-tuned versions of the family model's engine. Triumph chose an entirely different course for the Vitesse model which appeared in May 1962. This, apart from a quadruple headlamp arrangement and different grille which served as identification, looked otherwise exactly like a Herald, but under the bonnet featured a 1.6 litre six-cylinder power unit. This engine was a small-bored version of the Standard Vanguard Six 2 litre unit, with the smaller bores being advantageous in allowing water jacketing around all cylinders rather than the siamezed arrangements of the 2 litre. Otherwise, the 1.6 litre was substantially the same, retaining the Vanguard engine's major components such as the crankshaft, connecting rods, and the entire valve gear. Bore and stroke measurements were 66.75 mm x 76 mm, giving 1596 cc, and with twin Solex carburettors and a compression ratio of 8.75:1 the "six"

produced 70 nett bhp at 5000 rpm, and 110 lbs/ft torque at 2800 rpm. These figures, despite a weight penalty of more than 1 cwt over the Herald, guaranteed a very lively performance, and in fact the Vitesse would prove to be a near 90 mph car, and with the ability to reach 60 and 70 mph from rest in around 17 and 25 seconds. Based on that of the Herald, but with improved layshaft bearings, the gearbox also featured closed-up indirect

Datapanel: Triumph Herald, Herald S, Herald 1200, Herald 12/50

	Herald/Herald S	Herald 1200 (12/50)
Engine	4 cyl, ohv	4 cyl, ohv
Capacity	948 cc	1147 cc
Bore	63 mm	69.3 mm
Stroke	76 mm	76 mm
Compression ratio	8.0:1	8.0:1 (8.5:1)
Max BHP	34.5 nett @ 4500 rpm	39 nett @ 4500 rpm (51 nett @ 5200 rpm)
Max torque	48 lbs/ft @ 2750 rpm	60 lbs/ft @ 2250 rpm (63 lbs/ft @ 2600 rpm)
Gearing	13.3 mph/1000 rpm	15.7 mph/1000 rpm
Tyres	5.20 x 13	5.20 x 13
Kerb weight	16 cwt	16^{1}/4 cwt (16^{1}/2 cwt)
Overall length	12 ft 9 in	12 ft 9 in
Overall width	5 ft	5 ft
Wheelbase	7 ft 7^{1}/2 in	7 ft 7^{1}/2 in
Performance	"The Motor" R/T No. 12/59	"The Motor" R/T No. 6/64 (Herald 12/50)
Max speed		
Top gear	70.9 mph (mean) 72.6 mph (best)	77.5 mph (mean) 80.3 mph (best)
3rd gear	57 mph	65 mph
2nd gear	33 mph	53 mph
1st gear	not recorded	30 mph
Acceleration		
0–30 mph	7.2 seconds	5.5 seconds
0–50 mph	19.2 seconds	13.3 seconds
0–60 mph	31.1 seconds	21.3 seconds
0–70 mph	–	37.1 seconds
	Top gear/3rd gear	Top gear/3rd gear
20–40 mph	12.7/8.6 seconds	11.8/7.4 seconds
30–50 mph	15.1/11.9 seconds	12.9/8.6 seconds
40–60 mph	21.1/– seconds	17.2/13.6 seconds
50–70 mph	–/–	28.5/– seconds
Fuel consumption	34.5 mpg (1045 miles)	30.4 mpg (827 miles)

ratios. A 4.11:1 final drive ratio and 5.60 x 13 tyres gave overall gearing of 16.4 mph/1000 rpm.

Considerable stiffening of the chassis had been undertaken in order to cope with the heavier engine, whilst to tame the extra performance whenever necessary, the Vitesse was equipped with 9 inch diameter front disc brakes as standard, and rear drums of 1 inch greater diameter than on the Herald.

Anodised aluminium bumpers were making a first appearance on a British car with the announcement of the Vitesse, these being as a result of the availability of a new and very strong alloy recently developed by the British Aluminium Co. A contrasting colour stripe was another recognition feature, but otherwise, apart from the frontal treatment already mentioned, the Vitesse bodywork was as on the Herald. Apart from having a padded facia top, equipment and interior trim were also virtually identical, and the prices of £837 and £897 for the saloon and convertible Vitesse, respectively, reflected the engineering changes. Budget tax reductions had resulted in the corresponding Herald saloon and convertible now being listed at £660 and £731, respectively.

Early problems with water leaks at the joints of the Herald's bolted-up bodywork had by this time largely been solved, and several modifications had also been introduced to combat broken rear axle shafts which were not uncommon on early Heralds. Otherwise, the model had given few problems, and despite a slight price disadvantage over obvious rival cars was selling well.

A Herald 12/50 appeared in March 1963, having in addition to greater performance than the regular Herald 1200 which was continuing unchanged, the padded facia top of the Vitesse, and a Weathershields "Sunway" opening roof as standard equipment. An increase in compression ratio to 8.5:1, and the high-lift camshaft from the Triumph Spitfire sportscar which shared the same basic 1147 cc engine, were features which raised the power and torque outputs of the 12/50 model to 51 bhp at 5200 rpm and 63 lbs/ft at 2600 rpm. Front disc brakes, having been optional on the 1200 for some time past, were standardized on the 12/50, whilst unseen technical changes included an improved front propeller shaft joint, and a cast iron clutch bell housing with which to eliminate a resonance apparent with the previous aluminium cover. Further tax reductions had reduced the 948 cc Herald S model to £552, and the 1200 saloon to £579, above which the new 12/50 model came in at £635.

The 12/50's sunroof became optional equipment on the Vitesse saloon at this time, and in September 1963 both saloon and convertible Vitesse cars received improved instrumentation now including a rev-counter. During 1965 the Vitesse acquired a pair of Stromberg carburettors in place of the Solex instruments, and continued in its 1.6 litre from until late in 1966 when it became the Vitesse 2 litre upon being fitted with the 1998 cc engine from the Standard Vanguard's successor, the luxury Triumph 2000.

Meanwhile, during 1964 first the Herald S model, and much later in the year the 1200 Coupe were deleted, leaving the 1200 saloon, estate car, and convertible models, and the 12/50 saloon in production. Apart from minor changes, which included a diaphragm spring clutch being introduced early in 1966, this series now continued unaltered until August 1967 at which time the range went into Herald 13/60 form upon the adoption of a 1296 cc engine, and which was again a larger-bored version of the previous unit.

5

VAUXHALL

VICTOR, VX 4/90 FB SERIES

Although enjoying considerable sales success, Vauxhall's first F Series Victor model had met with some criticism in respect of both its styling and its susceptibility to serious corrosion at an early age, and so the rectification of these aspects was a priority at Luton during the design and development stages of the replacement car. Thus, the new bodyshell for the Victor FB Series, which appeared in September 1961, inherited nothing from its predecessor and bore no family resemblance whatsoever in its outward appearance. In the latter respect it was introducing a new, and very clean line for Vauxhall which broke away completely from the flamboyant nature of the company's 1950s products.

Slightly longer than that which it was replacing, this new bodyshell had the advantage of considerable underbody bracing, with an interesting arrangement whereby the longitudinal front and rear U-section members running both sides of the car tapered outwards under the passenger compartment to terminate centrally at the inner sill. Also situated beneath the floor, just above the gearbox position, was a transverse member of similar section, whilst another ran across the floorpan inside the car under the front seat. Cross bracing behind the rear seat squab was a further aid to overall rigidity. Complete underbody sealing, including wax injection for the sills, was applied during manufacture.

The wide bonnet top, hinged at its rear, gave excellent accessibility for routine checks, but was not self-supporting, being held open by means of a stay. The boot lid however was counterbalanced, and opened from boot floor level to reveal a usefully wide compartment. The spare wheel fitted neatly inside the right-hand rear wing where it was secured in an upright position by means of a strap. Occupying just a little space in the nearside wing was the petrol filler tube to the underfloor 10 gallon tank, which itself resided safely between the rear chassis-type members.

Although at 5 feet 4 inches only a $^1/_2$ inch wider overall than the previous model, the new Victor offered greater interior dimensions within a slightly lengthened wheelbase and wider track, and in its front bench seat/column gearchange form could now be regarded as a six-seater car. With three variants on offer, Standard, Super, and De Luxe, the interior appointments varied accordingly, with the Standard model appearing somewhat sparse with rubber floorcovering, a sunvisor for the driver only, and just a single horn operated by a steering wheel centre button. With carpeting, twin sunvisors, a hornring sounding dual horns, front door armrests, and a door

A pleasing continuity of line characterized the new FB series Victor. This beautifully-kept example was photographed in 1986.

A basic model was produced devoid of the bright metal window surrounds. Seen here in 1973 when approaching ten years of age, 7416 RH has had a set of wheeltrims added by some proud owner.

operated courtesy light, the Victor Super was much better equipped. Both these models featured PVC upholstery and front bench seat as standard, but with individual front seats as an extra-cost option, as was also the heater unit. Leather upholstery, individual front seats, heater, and windscreen washers were standard equipment on the top-of-the-range De Luxe car. On all three cars twin circular dials faced the driver, one being the speedometer with the other containing the fuel gauge and one for engine temperature. A lidded compartment faced the front seat passenger, but there was no parcel shelf.

Externally, chrome plated bumpers, grille, hubcaps, door handles, and side/tail lamp surrounds were common to all three models, with bright metal front and rear windscreen surrounds featuring on the Super and De Luxe cars rather than the rubber surrounds as on the Standard Victor. Bright

metal wheeltrims were an additional De Luxe feature, as was two tone paintwork if required.

Powering the new range was a very slightly modified version of the outgoing Victor's engine. This was the 1½ litre oversquare (79.4 mm x 76.2 mm) deep-skirt cylinder block unit which had given excellent service previously. Although retaining the single Zenith carburettor, the engine now featured a raised compression ratio of 8.1:1 (7.8:1 previously) and a correspondingly improved power output of 56.3 bhp (49.5 nett) at 4600 rpm by comparison with the earlier unit's 55 bhp at 4200 rpm. New, longer life aluminiumised exhaust valves, and a redesigned water pump were internal improvements, with the use of aluminium now for the timing case and clutch housing resulting in a usefully lighter engine unit overall.

The hydraulically operated clutch, and three-speed all synchromesh gearbox with steering column change were as before, but an important new option now was a four-speed all synchromesh gearbox with a remote control floor mounted lever. A propeller shaft of greater diameter than before was in the interests of improving drive-line smoothness at high cruising speeds, and was transmitting the power to a new final-drive assembly with a 3.9:1 ratio giving overall gearing of 17.3 mph/1000 rpm.

A recirculating ball steering box was retained, as was coil spring and wishbone independent front suspension which was now however mounted directly to the new bodyshell's longitudinal stiffeners rather than the previously separately attached crossmember. A transverse anti-roll bar linked the front suspension units. At the rear of the car a pair of longitudinally mounted four-leaf semi-elliptic springs located the live axle, with spring wind up under torque reaction being quite effectively controlled by arms protruding forward from the axle casing over the rear springs; rubber buffers at the forward end of these arms supplemented the usual rubber bump stops. Both front and rear springs were slightly softer than before, and completing the suspension were Vauxhall's own telescopic dampers fitted all round.

The Lockheed hydraulic braking system consisted of 8 inch diameter drums all round, with these housing shoes of a modest 92 square inches

Good design speaks for itself—and for you

VAUXHALL VICTOR ESTATE CAR

Memories are made of this. The Victor estate car was fine for pleasure trips too.

The high-performance VX 4/90 was always recognisable with its own grille and sideflash. TSV 729 is pictured recently amongst a number of other classic Vauxhalls.

VICT

total lining area. The 13 inch diameter, four-stud fixing roadwheels were equipped with 5.60 x 13 crossply tyres.

In all, this new Victor represented a very worthwhile development of the previous car, yet was being made available without any increase in price with £744, £781, and £847 being asked for the Standard, Super, and De Luxe models. Separate front seats on the two lower priced cars cost just £14/11s/8d extra, and for the excellent new four-speed gearbox there was only another £17/10s to pay.

Announced simultaneously, at a price of £861 which was actually £22 less than the preceding model was the new Victor Estate Car. This was a particularly neat adaptation which retained the saloon's elegant rear wing design, and featured a large counterbalanced lift up tailgate for luggage compartment access. Stiffer rear springs, 5.90 x 13 tyres of six-ply construction, and slightly lower gearing by courtesy of the 4.125:1 rear axle of the earlier Victor models were the technical changes necessary with which to cope with the greater loads possible.

The Victor saloon was in direct competition with the recently introduced Ford Classic listed at £796 and £825 in its four-door Basic and De Luxe configuration. With its maximum speed of around 76/77 mph, and requiring 24 seconds to reach 60 mph from rest, the Victor was only very marginally less quick than the rival Ford, and fuel economy in the 30 to 40 mpg category at touring speeds was also very similar. The Vauxhall was however offering slightly better passenger accommodation, particularly in respect of internal width, and its less bold but very clean and well-balanced styling was to prove more attractive to many eyes.

Promised at the Victor's launch, but not in fact going into production until February 1962, was a faster and more luxuriously equipped version to be known as the VX 4/90. Providing the considerably greater urge of this model was a suitably uprated version of the standard engine, with a light-alloy cylinder head of 9.3:1 compression ratio replacing the normal cast iron item, Twin Zenith downdraught carburettors were employed, whilst a camshaft of different profile gave an increase in both overlap and total valve opening time. These modifications resulted in 71.5 bhp (nett) at 5200 rpm, and to cope with this increase and the anticipated sustained use of high rpm came a new crankshaft forged from a tougher grade of steel.

The four-speed gearbox was standard, and with the adoption of 14 inch diameter roadwheels for this variant the overall gearing was raised slightly to 18.1 mph/1000 rpm on the standard 3.9:1 axle ratio. These new roadwheels were shod with 5.60 x 14 tyres, and were of five-stud fixing rather than the four-stud arrangements of the normal Victor's 13 inch rims. Behind the VX 4/90's front rims could be found $10\frac{1}{2}$ inch diameter Lockheed disc brakes which would more than match the extra performance on offer; vacuum servo assistance completed this uprated braking system. Giving an altogether more sporting bias to the handling qualities were road springs stiffer by more than 30 per cent, with which the VX 4/90 would enjoy appreciably more level cornering capabilities than the softer sprung and somewhat roll-prone Victor.

Inside, a new "two way stretch" plastic material covered the seats, which included the individual front seat arrangement as standard; a centre armrest made its appearance now in the rear. The door trims in the front included large map pockets, and all four doors featured imitation wood inserts just below window level. This wood-grain was also applied to the facia, and a small parcel shelf below the glove box was to be another exclusive VX 4/90 feature. A rev-counter now occupied the circular housing alongside the speedometer, with these two large instruments now being flanked by four

A new grille identified the 1.6 litre Victors which came in 1963, and is shown here on a brochure cover illustration.

Leather seating and pile
carpeting with underlay
were features of the
inviting interior of the
Victor De Luxe, and . . .

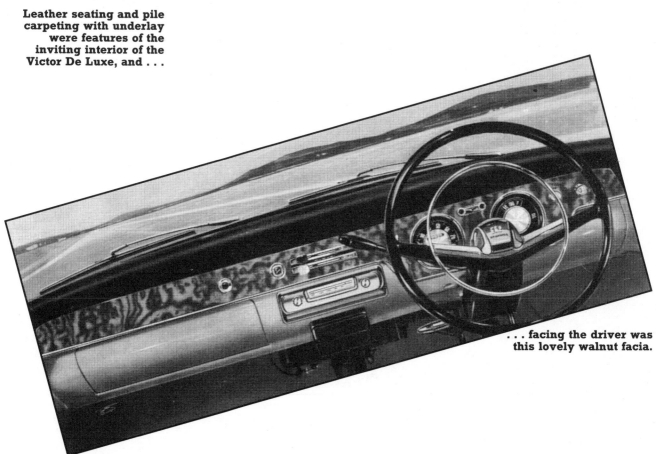

. . . facing the driver was
this lovely walnut facia.

A constant-depth
sideflash identified the
1.6 litre VX 4/90, as seen
here with the optional
radio, wing mirrors, spot
and fog lights.

smaller dials accommodating an ammeter, fuel gauge, oil pressure gauge,
and that for engine temperature.

A contrastingly coloured side "flash", its own exclusive grille and
wheeltrim rings, and different tail lamp treatment were the external features
identifying the VX 4/90. Capable of almost 90 mph, and able to reach 60 and
70 mph from rest in 17 and 23 seconds, the VX 4/90 was in addition to its
extra luxuries a usefully quicker car than the lower order Victors, and at
£984 was continuing the good value for money theme of this Vauxhall series
as a whole.

Being "right", right from the start, the FB range therefore continued
virtually unchanged throughout 1962, enhancing Vauxhall's reputation
considerably as it came into widespread ownership.

A change in specification came in the summer of 1963 when the entire
range, particularly the lesser models, were endowed with greater all round
performance. Larger cylinder bores, now 81.6 mm, in conjunction with the
same 76.2 mm stroke as before raised the swept volume to 1594 cc. With a

157

An exclusive seating arrangement, walnut door cappings, and extra instrumentation were VX 4/90 features. The conveniently-placed gearlever, and equally convenient handbrake are nice practical touches.

This brochure illustration of the VX 4/90 also recalls Vauxhall's past, with a legendary Prince Henry Vauxhall of 1912 appearing in the background.

Datapanel: Vauxhall FB Series Victor VX 4/90

	Victor 1.5 (1.6 litre)	VX 4/90 1.5 (1.6 litre)
Engine	4 cyl, ohv	4 cyl, ohv
Capacity	1508 cc (1594 cc)	1508 cc (1594 cc)
Bore	79.3 mm (81.6 mm)	79.3 mm (81.6 mm)
Stroke	76.2 mm	76.2 mm
Compression ratio	8.0:1 (8.5:1)	9.3:1
Max BHP	49.5 @ 4600 rpm (58.5 @ 4600 rpm)	71.5 @ 5200 rpm (73.8 @ 5200 rpm)
Max torque	85.6 lbs/ft @ 2200 rpm (84.3 lbs/ft @ 2400 rpm)	91 lbs/ft @ 2800 rpm (98.7 lbs/ft @ 3200 rpm)
Gearing	17.5 mph/1000 rpm (16.5 mph/1000 rpm)	18.1 mph/1000 rpm
Tyres	5.60 x 13	5.60 x 14
Kerb weight	19^1/4 cwt	19^3/4 cwt
Overall length	14 ft 5^1/4 in	14 ft 5^1/4 in
Overall width	5 ft 4in	5 ft 4 in
Wheelbase	8 ft 4 in	8 ft 4 in
Performance	"Autocar" 23rd November 1962 Victor Super 1508 cc	"Autocar" 16th March 1962 VX 4/90 1508 cc
Max speed		
Top gear	76.5 mph (mean) 77.0 mph (best)	88.0 mph (mean) 88.0 mph (best)
3rd gear	69 mph	72 mph
2nd gear	45 mph	46 mph
1st gear	29 mph	30 mph
Acceleration		
0–30 mph	5.8 seconds	4.9 seconds
0–50 mph	14.9 seconds	11.6 seconds
0–60 mph	23.4 seconds	16.9 seconds
0–70 mph	36.5 seconds	23.0 seconds
	Top gear/3rd gear	Top gear/3rd gear
20–40 mph	11.6/8.4 seconds	14.6/9.2 seconds
30–50 mph	12.9/9.9 seconds	11.8/8.1 seconds
40–60 mph	15.9/13.9 seconds	13.4/9.6 seconds
50–70 mph	24.6/– seconds	16.7/11.9 seconds
Fuel consumption	28.0 mpg (1003 miles)	24.2 mpg (1026 miles)

compression ratio now of 8.5:1 the Victor engines developed 58 bhp (nett) at 4800 rpm. This 20 per cent improvement in power output was accompanied by lower overall gearing now of 16.5 mph/1000 rpm, as the estate's car's axle ratio of 4.125:1 was being standardized on all but the VX 4/90. A larger diameter clutch accompanied the increase in engine size, but the three- and four-speed gearboxes remained as before. Larger, 9 inch diameter front brake drums were introduced to cope with the extra performance, and for the hard-driving Victor owner now was the option of the VX 4/90 front disc/rear drum system at an extra cost of £21/10s which included the provision of the VX 4/90's 14 inch wheels.

A redesigned grille, now of polished aluminium rather than the earlier chrome plated fitting identified these latest Victors, and there was restyled interior trim with the De Luxe model receiving a walnut facia.

Victors could now just exceed 80 mph, and accelerate from rest to 60 and 70 mph in around 18 and 29 seconds. The combination of a larger capacity engine and slightly lower gearing also improved the flexibility, with the Victors also now displaying usefully quicker top-gear performance. The inevitable cost of this, due in most part to the lower ratio final drive, was a slight increase in fuel consumption under most conditions, although with a 32/33 mpg figure at a constant 50 mph a Victor was still by no means thirsty. The increase in engine capacity gave only a small improvement in power output, now 74 bhp nett, on the already highly-tuned VX 4/90, and as this retained the 3.9:1 axle the improvements in speed and acceleration were such as to really need a stopwatch to detect. Constant speed fuel consumption figures however did show worthwhile gains, with the VX 4/90 now proving rather better than the lower-geared Victors in this respect.

Purchase tax reductions sometime previously had more than offset a small earlier manufacturer's price increase, with the updated FB range now being listed at £635 (Standard), £667 (Super), £723 (De Luxe), and £840 for the VX 4/90. At these prices the FB Series continued into 1964, selling alongside such as the Austin A60 Cambridge at £721, and Ford's new Corsair which in four-door basic and De Luxe forms was £677 and £701. At £840 the Corsair 1500GT matched the VX 4/90 on price exactly. Despite this sort of opposition however the FB Vauxhalls continued to broaden their well-deserved popularity, and it was with some surprise to many that this successful line was replaced for 1965 with the mechanically similar, but totally rebodied Victor 101.

VELOX, CRESTA PB SERIES

A very strong family resemblance to the FB Victor was the immediate visual impression created by the new PB Series Velox and Cresta upon their debut in October 1962, with Vauxhall's new look suiting these large six-seater cars particularly well.

Very slightly longer and wider, at 15 feet 1³/4 inches and 5 feet 10¹/2 inches overall, and on a longer wheelbase now of 8 feet 11¹/2 inches (8 feet 9 in previously) than the outgoing PA Series, this latest range featured a completely new bodyshell. Structurally, as well as in appearance, this could be seen as virtually a scaling up of the successful FB Victor body. Included was a similar underbody bracing layout in which the longitudinal members running from the front and rear extremities each splayed outwards to meet the inner sill at its centre point. A substantial transverse stiffener ran beneath the front seats. Cross bracing behind the rear seat squab and, unlike on the new Victor now, a back panel appreciably above boot floor level were further aids to rigidity.

A 10³/4 gallon fuel tank was situated transversely behind the rear seat as in the preceding Velox/Cresta, with the spare wheel also remaining in its horizontal position in a well in the boot floor as on the earlier cars; both the boot lid and bonnet top were counterbalanced. Unlike on the PA models however, and in keeping with the new Victor again, the front wings were now unstressed bolt-on items, the body was devoid of mud traps whilst the

The glamorous nature of big-car motoring is emphasized in this brochure cover illustration of the new PB series Velox.

Whitewall tyres, wheeltrims, and a moulding applied to the shoulder line serve to identify the top-of-the-range Cresta in this Vauxhall publicity picture. The family likeness to the smaller Victor is perhaps most readily apparent in a side view.

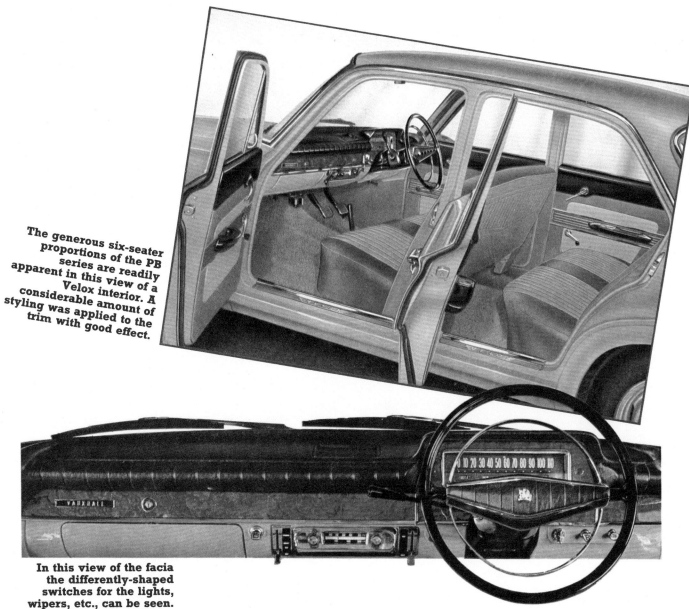

sills, ventilated to avoid moisture build up, were injected with a polythene wax. Final underbody treatment was a coating of bituminous plastic.

Of greater structural rigidity, and appreciably roomier, this bodyshell was nevertheless said to be almost 40 lbs lighter than its predecessor the PA model. Over an extended period it was to prove notably more rust resistant also, thus playing its part in achieving everything Vauxhall set out to offer with this model.

Serving only to highlight the elegant styling were bright metal embellishments applied with some discretion. These consisted of the window surrounds, door handles, grille, headlamp rims, sidelamp surrounds and bumpers; additional on the Cresta only were wheeltrims and a full length strip at shoulder height.

Four large doors gave very easy access to a generously sized passenger compartment, this featuring bench seats both front and rear fully in keeping with the six-seater claim. Deeply sprung, these were in Vynide on the Velox only, with either leather or a nylon cloth to choice on the Cresta. On the latter, pull-down armrests appeared in both front and rear compartments, but on the rear seat only as standard in the Velox with one for the front

163

being an optional extra. Seats and door trims were in dual tones, and all four doors were equipped with combined armrest/doorpulls, with those in the rear each incorporating an ashtray. Fitted carpets covered the floor, and both cars featured the same facia which included a full-width burr-walnut panel running beneath the padded top. Set into the walnut on the driver's side was the horizontal ribbon type speedometer with which, as on the previous model a moving band of colour changed from green to orange at 30 mph, and from orange to red when the car's speed reached the mile-a-minute rate. Other instrumentation was confined to a total mileage recorder, engine temperature and fuel tank contents gauges. The instruments were viewed through a large diameter steering wheel complete with full circle hornring and safety-padded spokes.

Heating and demisting arrangements were once again standard on the Cresta only, whilst remaining as optional equipment on the Velox. An electric clock, screenwashers, underbonnet sound insulation, fog and spot lamps, and twin reversing lamps were other standard Cresta items.

The smooth running, square, (82.55 mm x 82.55 mm) in-line six-cylinder unit of 2651 cc which had powered late examples of the PA Vauxhalls was continued now with only minor changes. Of the pushrod operated overhead valve type, this engine featured a deep skirt cylinder block with widely spaced bore centres, and a four main bearing crankshaft with generously sized bearing surfaces. The single Zenith carburettor was retained, but an increase in compression ratio to 8.5:1 (8.0:1 previously), and a mildly reprofiled camshaft suggested that a little more power than hitherto would be available. However, somewhat surprisingly, Vauxhall continued to quote the earlier model's figures for this latest car. These were 95 bhp nett at 4600 rpm, and 128 lbs ft of torque at a mere 1600 rpm which confirmed that these latest big Vauxhalls would once again be extremely flexible cars.

The 8½ inch diameter clutch was new, now being of the diaphragm-spring type, and operated by a mechanical linkage rather than the hydraulic arrangements of the preceding Velox/Cresta range. The all synchromesh three-speed gearbox was as before, and again with the steering column mounted gearchange lever. To this could be added a switch controlled Laycock overdrive which operated on second and top gears, and when specified came in conjunction with the 3.9:1 axle ratio of the preceding models with which it gave a usefully spaced five-speed arrangement. The standard axle ratio was now 3.7:1, giving 19.3 mph/1000 rpm on top gear, and was also employed with the automatic transmission option. As before, the automatic gearbox was the General Motors Hydro-Matic three-speed unit which featured torque multiplication on first and reverse gears only. Manual selection of the low and intermediate ratios was also provided for with this gearbox in addition to its fully automatic operation.

Bolted through rubber insulators to the body's longitudinal members at the front was a transverse platform carrying the independent front suspension units. These were of the coil spring and wishbone type once again, and with Vauxhall's usual double-acting telescopic dampers. An anti-roll torsion bar linked the two independent suspension assemblies. The Burman recirculating ball steering box controlled the direction of the front wheels via a three-piece trackrod arrangement, with the entire steering gear being behind the front axle line.

At the rear, long leaf springs of just three leaves each were shackled at their extremities to the rear underbody longitudinal members, and attached to the rigid rear axle well forward of their centre. As on the Victor, forward protruding arms from the axle casing were employed to limit any wind-up

tendencies, and inward-angled telescopic dampers completed the arrangements here.

The Lockheed braking system now included the previously optional front disc brakes as standard equipment. Of $10\frac{1}{2}$ inches diameter, these discs were in conjunction with 9 inch diameter by $1\frac{3}{4}$ inch wide drums at the rear, and with servo-assistance also being a standard feature. The 14 inch diameter roadwheels had 5.90 x 14 crossply tyres, with those of the Cresta incorporating a white sidewall band.

Although introduced at prices of £936 (Velox) and £1046 (Cresta), a purchase tax reduction almost immediately afterwards reduced car prices across the board, bringing the new Vauxhalls down to an attractive £822 and £919; an extra £133 would buy the automatic gearbox option. At these levels the big Vauxhalls were once again in direct competition with Ford's similar offerings, the Zephyr 6 (£837), and the Zodiac Mk 3 at £971, and were offering virtually identical passenger accommodation and, broadly speaking, very similar performance too. The new Vauxhall's ability to reach 70 and 80 mph from rest in around 20 and 30 seconds was rather better than the Zephyr 6, whilst falling a little short of the slightly more powerful Zodiac which also had the advantage of a 100 mph maximum speed. Nevertheless, allied to the PB's useful acceleration was a near 95 mph maximum, and with a fuel consumption in the 20 to 25 mpg bracket, and that slight price advantage over the rival Fords at this time they were very well placed to take a good share of the market for this type of car.

Estate car variants of the big Vauxhalls became available in October 1963, these being Vauxhall-approved conversions of the saloons carried out by Martin Walter Ltd., of Folkestone. A steel-framed fibreglass roof extension was invisibly blended in to the saloon, and the wide counterbalanced lift up tailgate was also a fibreglass moulding. The rear passenger doors, with their squared up window frames were straight from the Victor estate car; aft of these were full size windows leaving only very slim pillars at the rear. A folding rear passenger seat was now provided, allowing a maximum 6 feet 1

165

A double-page spread announcing the 3.3 litre models. It only needs to be added here that it's all true – you really could get all of this for less than £1000.

inch load length when the squab was down; 4 feet 2 inches remained with the seat-back raised. The compartment's width was reduced slightly by comparison with that of the normal saloon's boot as the spare wheel was now located in an upright position in the offside, this re-arrangement being necessary to allow an underfloor fuel tank in the estate car.

Despite a modest weight penalty the performance remained unchanged, thus suggesting that perhaps the aerodynamic properties of the estate car were rather better than on the corresponding saloon. Priced at £1203 and £1305 for the Velox and Cresta, the estate cars were undercut by the rival Ford Zephyr 6 (£1115) and Zodiac (£1249) estates, but could nevertheless be still considered as good value in their own right.

A Vauxhall price increase sometime previously had resulted in saloon prices now of £840 and £943, and these levels were maintained for a further year until October 1964 when changes to the PB range were announced.

halls

A considerably larger capacity engine was the most interesting aspect of the PB's revised specification. An arrangement whereby the outer walls of adjacent cylinders were flat at their closest to each other allowed greater internal bore diameter whilst retaining water jacketing between them. The stroke remained the same, with bore sizes now of 92 mm (82.55 mm previously) being solely responsible for an increase in capacity from 2651 cc to 3293 cc. In conjunction with the same cylinder head casting as before were new pistons featuring a depression in the crown with which to maintain the 8.5:1 compression ratio as before. Valve seats cut at a greater angle allowed improved passages in the cylinder head, and larger exhaust valves were now employed. The single Zenith carburettor was now of greater choke tube diameter, and a dual exhaust system was introduced to get the gases away.

All of this resulted in 115 bhp nett at 4200 rpm, and a torque curve now peaking at 2200 rpm at which a massive 175 lbs ft torque was being produced, these figures promising quite exceptional acceleration.

The three-speed column-controlled gearbox remained as the standard transmission, but with raised first and second gears more appropriate to the greater power, whilst a new option now was an all synchromesh four-speed gearbox with direct-acting floor change mechanism. Relatively high, and nicely spaced indirect ratios were an excellent feature of this new gearbox, but with which overdrive however was not available, although that particular item of equipment could still be specified with the regular three-speed gearbox. On the automatic cars the Hydra-Matic was now giving way to General Motors Powerglide transmission which differed considerably from the earlier gearbox in that it only consisted of two forward speeds, but now providing torque multiplication on the highest ratio. The 3.7:1 final drive was standard now with whichever transmission arrangements were chosen.

A new full width grille, now embracing the headlamps, identified these latest PB models, with the Cresta additionally acquiring a full length chrome strip running just above wheelarch level; the previous shoulder height strip was deleted at this time.

Separate front seats could now be specified, at £8/9/2d with fixed

More than twenty years on, and still looking great, one of the powerful PB Crestas poses quietly at a Classic Car gathering.

Datapanel: Vauxhall PB Series Velox/Cresta

	2.6 litre	3.3 litre
Engine	6 cyl, ohv	6 cyl, ohv
Capacity	2651 cc	3294 cc
Bore	82.55 mm	96.1 mm
Stroke	82.55 mm	82.55 mm
Compression ratio	8.5:1	8.5:1
Max BHP	95 @ 4600 rpm	115 nett @ 4200 rpm
Max torque	128 lbs/ft @ 1600 rpm	175 lbs/ft @ 2200 rpm
Gearing	19.3 mph/1000 rpm	19.3 mph/1000 rpm (20.7 mph/1000 rpm later)
Tyres	5.90 x 14	5.90 x 14
Kerb weight	24 cwt	24 cwt
Overall length	15 ft 1^3/$_4$ in	15 ft 1^3/$_4$ in
Overall width	5 ft 10^1/$_2$ in	5 ft 10^1/$_2$ in
Wheelbase	8 ft 11^1/$_2$ in	8 ft 11^1/$_2$ in
Performance	"Autocar" 11th January 1963 Cresta (Hydra-Matic)	"Motor" R/T No. 13/65 Cresta (3.7 axle)
Max speed		
Top gear	90.5 mph (mean) 93.0 mph (best)	97.5 mph (mean) 101.1 mph (best)
3rd gear	–	71.5 mph
2nd gear	59 mph	54.5 mph
1st gear	34 mph	38.5 mph
Acceleration		
0–30 mph	5.2 seconds	3.6 seconds
0–50 mph	11.5 seconds	7.2 seconds
0–60 mph	16.8 seconds	10.6 seconds
0–70 mph	24.1 seconds	14.7 seconds
0–80 mph	36.1 seconds	21.0 seconds
	Top gear/2nd gear	Top gear/3rd gear
20–40 mph	–/6.3 seconds	5.7/4.5 seconds
30–50 mph	10.7/6.7 seconds	5.9/4.5 seconds
40–60 mph	12.1/– seconds	6.5/4.9 seconds
50–70 mph	13.9/– seconds	8.0/7.2 seconds
60–80 mph	19.3/–	10.0/– seconds
Fuel consumption	18.3 mpg (1234 miles)	17.0 mpg (1350 miles)

backrests, or £30 with reclining squabs. Only a slight price increase overall covered the improvements introduced, with £859 and £962 being asked for what were by a considerable margin now the liveliest cars in the family six-cylinder class. An ability to reach 90 mph from rest through the gears in less than 30 seconds was accompanied by outstanding top gear acceleration too, although the maximum speed still fell a little short of a genuine two-way 100 mph.

With the larger engine pulling the same gearing the fuel consumption figures showed an inevitable increase, with little more than 20 mpg being possible even when only leisurely progress was being made. Rectifying this situation somewhat, early in 1965, came a raised axle ratio of 3.45:1, giving 20.7 mph/1000 rpm on top gear and a 2 to 3 mpg improvement at touring speeds, and with barely any reduction in the car's remarkable accelerative powers.

Power assisted steering for the first time on a Vauxhall became an option, at £60 extra cost, also early in 1965, after which the PB Series continued without further changes until deleted late in the year when the rebodied PC Series Cresta and Cresta De Luxe were announced for 1966.

VIVA HA SERIES

Having thoroughly updated their medium and large car models, Vauxhall then expanded their range with the addition of a completely new car. This was the HA Series Viva, and was the company's first entry since the war into the hotly contested small-car market.

After studying the possibilities of a front-wheel-drive layout, and alternatively a rear-engined model, Vauxhall nevertheless decided upon the well proven front-engine rear-wheel-drive configuration; low first cost coupled with reliability were prime considerations, and could be virtually guaranteed by this conventional design approach.

The basis of the new car was a two-door monocoque bodyshell in which styling considerations came secondary to those of comfortable passenger accommodation, and very ample luggage space. Thus, the Viva was to be characterized by a somewhat boxy appearance, but which was nevertheless well proportioned. Underbody bracing consisted of a full length box member running longitudinally at either side, stiffened sills, and a transverse member beneath both the front and rear seat positions. A diagonal member running across the framework behind the rear seat squab also contributed to the overall rigidity, as did a rear back panel appreciably higher than boot floor level.

The wide passenger doors were each equipped with wind down main windows and separate swivelling quarter window. Both front seats tipped forward to facilitate entry to the rear bench seat which, despite some wheelarch intrusion was of very ample width for two persons; recessed armrests in the rear side trim panels were a feature adding to the comfort of those travelling in the rear. The seats were upholstered in a combination of rayon cloth and Vynide, with the latter material being confined to the upper part of the squab and seat side panels only. The door trims and rear interior panels were also in Vynide, whilst the floorcovering was rubber matting in the basic model, with carpets being a feature of the De Luxe car. Other De Luxe model amenities were the provision of the heater as standard, opening rear side windows, door-operated interior light, a passenger's sunvisor, ashtrays, and windscreen washers.

The painted metal facia panel was complete with a padded top, and contained two large circular instruments immediately ahead of the driver, one of which being the speedometer and distance recorder whilst the other housed the fuel gauge and warning lights for ignition and low oil pressure. These were viewed directly through the upper half of the deeply dished steering wheel. Rocker switches to the right of the instruments controlled the windscreen wipers, and the head and sidelamps, with the headlamp dipping and flashing facility being operated by a steering column mounted

The Viva's family-car role, its economy and value are emphasized in this brochure illustration.

That squarish shape resulted in a very roomy small car. The text accompanying this advertisement stresses the durability of the Viva's well-protected bodywork.

multi-purpose stalk which also took care of the horn and direction indicators. Running beneath the facia was a full width parcel shelf with a padded front edge, and deep enough to accommodate the optional radio.

The full width, rear hinged bonnet top was supported in the open position by means of a simple stay, whereas at the rear of the car the equally wide boot lid was self-supporting. Very conveniently shaped, and large for this class of car, the luggage compartment housed the petrol tank in an upright position immediately aft of the wheelarch on the left, with the spare wheel occupying a similar position on the right.

In respect of its external appearance, the Viva was notable for its paintwork, being the first British car to feature an acrylic finish which, it was claimed, was resistant to atmospheric pollution to such a degree that it would never need polishing. Complimenting the paintwork were bright metal embellishments consisting of chrome plated bumper bars, hubcaps, and door handles, with the simple front grille being in aluminium.

Additionally, on the De Luxe, was a full length aluminium side trim running just beneath the window line, whilst chrome-effect plastic inserts were featured in the front and rear screen surrounds. Underbody and wheelarch protection consisted of a thick coating of bituminous paint, with a similar protection being applied to the inside of the sills during manufacture.

A completely new, 1057 cc capacity overhead valve engine powered the Viva, and was of considerably oversquare design with bore and stroke measurements of 74.3 mm x 60.96 mm. The compact, cast-iron cylinder block extended downwards only to the crankshaft centre-line, but was notable for such a compact unit that by virtue of being a thin-wall casting it provided water jacketing around each individual cylinder. Autothermic pistons were fitted, with three piston rings each, of which the top one was chrome plated. A forged steel crankshaft ran in three white metal main bearings, these being of a very ample $2\frac{1}{8}$ inch diameter; lead bronze was used for the big-end bearing shells, with the crankshaft journals here having a diameter of 1.77 inches.

The cylinder head departed from past Vauxhall practice in that its combustion chambers were of wedge shape, and so bringing these Vauxhalls into line with other General Motors products in this respect. Fully machined to extremely close tolerances, the combustion chambers gave a compression ratio of 8.5:1. Eliminating the more usual rocker shaft, the overhead valve gear featured pressed-steel rockers each of which being ball-jointed to individual stud mountings. An AC mechanical fuel pump

VAUXHALL VIVA

Viva value is *lasting* value—with seven stage rust-proofing of all body metal; deep primer dip for inside-out panel protection: door sills are painted *on the inside*: complete under-body seal at the factory at no extra charge. Baked-on primer, baked-on colour, baked-on "Magic Mirror" *acrylic* lacquer. The radiator grille is polished aluminium. This Viva is built to keep its value and its looks.

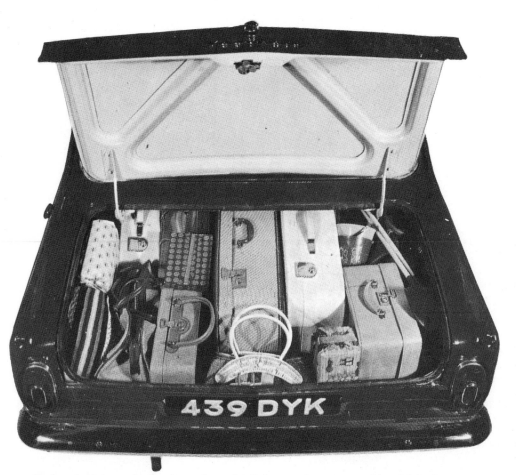

The roominess extended to the rear luggage compartment. The spare wheel is situated inside the offside wing, and only a minimal amount of baggage would need to be removed in order to gain access in the event of a punctured tyre.

supplied petrol to a single downdraught Solex carburettor, with which the new engine developed 44 bhp at 5000 rpm, and a maximum torque output of 59 lbs ft at 2800 rpm.

A diaphragm clutch was an up-to-the-minute feature, but displayed a marked cheapness in that it was cable operated at a time when hydraulic operation was still the norm even on inexpensive cars. Penny-pinching was avoided however in respect of the four-speed gearbox which was complete with synchromesh engagement throughout; a floor mounted remote control lever was provided for gear selection, and was to earn much praise for its extremely light and precise movement.

An open propeller shaft linked the gearbox to a short torque tube drive to the rear axle. With this beam axle/torque tube arrangement the suspension movements are limited to the torque tube only, leaving the propeller shaft to operate in a constant plane and therefore requiring only a very low transmission tunnel in the passenger compartment floor. The hypoid bevel final drive assembly of 4.125:1 ratio gave overall gearing of 15 mph/1000 rpm on top gear.

Of a basically conventional nature, the running gear nevertheless displayed some novelties. New to Vauxhall was rack and pinion steering gear, with the rubber-mounted rack being ahead of the front axle line. A turning circle of around 28 ft was excellent, but requiring $3^3/4$ turns of the steering wheel between the extremes of lock indicated a surprisingly low-geared set up for a light car.

Carried by a crossmember bolted through rubber insulators to the underside of the car, the independent front suspension utilised a conventional transverse upper and lower wishbone arrangement at each side, but otherwise differed considerably from the usual set-ups in that a single transverse leaf spring replaced the normal pair of coils. Each of the spring's three leaves were separated along their entire length by a series of rubber spacers; therefore, the interleaf friction which can give rise to some inconsistency in leaf spring operation was eliminated, and the system was claimed to be just as effective as a two coil spring and separate anti-roll bar installation, but at usefully lower cost.

At the rear, longitudinally mounted semi-elliptic leaf springs were attached somewhat ahead of their centres to forward protrusions from the axle casing, and therefore ahead of the axle line. With the axle pivoting at the forward end of the torque tube, the slightly forward spring mounting point travelled less than the axle/wheel centres during those conditions when both rear wheels moved upwards or downwards together, and this leverage had the effect of reducing the spring stiffness during these movements. This effect was not apparent under conditions of roll when one wheel rises as the other moves downward, therefore adequate roll stiffness was maintained. Vauxhall's own-designed telescopic shock absorbers completed the Viva's suspension.

A Girling hydraulic braking system was employed, with 8 inch diameter drums all round and a total lining area of 62.8 square inches. This seemed adequate enough for a 14 cwt car capable of 75 mph or so, but nevertheless, front disc brakes, complete with servo assistance were to be available as an extra-cost option. 12 inch diameter roadwheels were the smallest to appear on a Vauxhall so far, and were equipped with 5.50 x 12 crossply tyres.

Making its appearance in October 1963, at just £528 for the basic model, and £566 for the De Luxe, the Viva was immediately seen to be offering very competitive value in the small-car class along side such as BMC's Austin A40 at £556 for the basic model, and the Ford Anglia De Luxe at £538. With an ability to reach 60 mph from a standing start in 22 seconds, and to usefully exceed 75 mph flat out the Viva was also very competitive in

The jet fighter-plane theme used for the background of this 1964 advertisement serves to suggest that the Viva was an up-to-the-minute car. Although styled quite differently from the Victor and Velox ranges in almost every respect, the Viva did include very similar wheelarch and body-sill visual treatment in its design as on its larger stablemates.

173

terms of sheer performance. This was accompanied by a touring fuel consumption in the 35 to 45 mpg region, and even the hardest driving was unlikely to produce figures as low as 30 mpg, and with these attributes it was no surprise that this new Vauxhall quicky gained widespread popularity.

For an all-new design, the Viva was to prove remarkably trouble free, and requiring little in the way of revision to the basic specification. A filter for the carburettor pilot jet cured a tendency for the engine to idle unevenly on very early models; a stronger detent spring in the 1st/2nd gear synchromesh assembly eliminated the "crash" sometimes occuring when changing between these two ratios, again on very early cars.

A Viva-based van followed into production, marketed under the Bedford label, and an estate car variant of this was soon being produced as a conversion by coachbuilders Martin Walter, and still marketed as a Bedford but with the model name Beagle being added. This retained the van's twin rear doors, but was now complete with full length side windows, including a swivelling panel on either side. A pair of rear passenger seats were provided, and with these folded flat there was a 59 inch long rear loading platform, and as the van bodywork was some 5 inches taller than the Viva saloon, the cargo space was usefully greater than would have been the case had the conversion been carried out on the car. Stronger road springs allowed an 8 cwt payload, and a reduced compression ratio engine (7.3:1) enabled the Beagle to be operated on low-grade petrol.

Criticisms from some quarters regarding the Viva's low-geared and, in the opinion of some, over-light steering, were attended to by raising the steering gear ratio 20 per cent in September 1964. An improved silencer reducing exhaust system resonance was fitted to the De Luxe Viva from about this time also. Regarded as a much greater improvement was redesigned seating in which occupants were held more securely for the 1965 models.

The unburstable nature of the Viva engine had quickly lead to outside concerns offering tuning equipment, and a complete Viva GT model including suspension and interior modifications became available from LawrenceTune during 1964. This model featured a reworked cylinder head with a 10.0:1 compression ratio, a twin-choke Solex carburettor, and a three-branch exhaust manifold. This set-up raised the maximum speed to more than 85 mph whilst knocking 5 seconds or so off the 0 – 60 mph time, and coping with these increases was stiffened suspension which was also lowered by 2 inches all round. This was not an inexpensive conversion however, in fact costing a hefty £147 for the engine and suspension modifications alone, with extras such as a sports steering wheel and competition seats also available at further cost.

This was quickly followed by another 'outside job'', the Brabham Viva GT, developed by Brabham Conversions Ltd., the company headed by 1959/60 World Champion Racing Driver Jack Brabham. For £139 this conversion included a much modified cylinder head of 10.0:1 compression ratio, larger valves, and a twin Stromberg carburettor set-up. 60 bhp at 5800 rpm was the result of all this, which endowed the Viva with an almost 90 mph capability in addition to a 15 seconds 0 – 60 mph time. Lowered and stiffened suspension was also a part of this package.

Not quite matching these in performance, but nevertheless offering a useful increase came Vauxhall's own uprated Viva in October 1965 when a "90" engine option became available. This featured a 9.0:1 compression ratio, larger valves, and a single Stromberg carburettor in place of the standard model's Solex. 53 bhp at 5600 rpm was developed by this unit, putting the maximum speed up to rather more than 80 mph whilst shaving around 2 seconds from the 0 – 60 mph capability. The disc brake option was included whenever the uprated engine was specified, making the £28 extra cost for a Viva 90 very reasonable indeed.

An SL, "Super Luxury" package, at £41 extra was also introduced at this time, offering the buyer an appreciably better equipped Viva than hitherto. This consisted of internally, improved seats, now with foam overlay and covered in soft Ambla plastic, under carpet sound-deadening material, a lockable compartment under the facia, an engine temperature gauge, and twin horns. Identifying an SL model externally was a contrasting "flash" of

Book your seats now for the most exciting 1-litre performance of the year.

NEW VIVA 90. BY VAUXHALL

If you already like the look and feel of the Viva, but want a car with more power, this is it. The new Viva 90 opens up a totally new dimension in 1-litre family motoring, and is engineered from start to finish for high performance—to give you all the power you need at every speed—matched by power brakes with front discs. 60 brake horse power—20% more than the regular Viva—*and that one doesn't loiter!*

From a standing start the Viva 90 reaches 60 m.p.h. in 18.8 seconds. In top, real top gear performance— 40-60 m.p.h. in 14.5 seconds. And a jubilant maximum around 85 m.p.h.

The Viva 90 engine was built to complement the already magnificent handling qualities of the Viva. Snap-action 4-speed all-synchro gears with a handy short-throw lever. Light, responsive steering. Sports car cornering. The result — a perfectly balanced car. First-rate performance with sensational acceleration.

You can recognise the New Viva 90 by the gleaming "90" on the boot, the up-to-100 m.p.h. speedometer, and the bright red engine under the bonnet.

Call your Vauxhall dealer for a test drive. There's never been performance to touch the new Viva 90 in a 1-litre family car.

Is this the year you own a Viva?

The Viva 90 comes in two versions

Viva 90 de Luxe—Vynide upholstery, heater, screenwasher, headlamp flasher etc., £606.18.9

Viva 90 SL—the super lu... the dashing sideflash, Ambla Super Luxury features. £648...

Regular Viva prices start at £528...

A snappier performance in addition to the Viva's other established virtues was the exciting prospect for anyone buying a Viva 90.

Caught by the camera in 1984, KAX 204D appears to be a remarkably original example of the Viva SL 90.

colour along the body sides, restyled grille, bumper overriders, and wheeltrim rings.

All Viva engines now featured improved crankshaft bearings, whilst the range was also now benefiting from slight changes in the rear axle location in order to combat a tendency towards axle tramp under some conditions. With a range now consisting of the standard model, standard 90, De Luxe, De Luxe 90, SL, and SL 90, at prices ranging from £528 to £648 the Viva was to continue in production, and sell extremely well for a further year before being replaced by the almost wholly redesigned HB model in October 1966.

Datapanel: Vauxhall	HA Series	Viva	Viva SL90
		Viva	Viva S190
Engine		4 cyl, ohv	4 cyl, ohv
Capacity		1057 cc	1057 cc
Bore		74.3 mm	74.3 mm
Stroke		61.0 mm	61.0 mm
Compression ratio		8.5:1	9.0:1
Max BHP		44 @ 5000 rpm	54 @ 5400 rpm
Max torque		59 lbs/ft @ 2800 rpm	65 lbs/ft @ 3200 rpm
Gearing		15 mph/1000 rpm	15 mph/1000 rpm
Tyres		5.50 x 12	5.50 x 12
Kerb weight		14$^{1}/_{2}$ cwt	14$^{1}/_{2}$ cwt
Overall length		13 ft 1$^{3}/_{4}$ in	13 ft 1$^{3}/_{4}$ in
Overall width		4 ft 11$^{1}/_{2}$ in	4 ft 11$^{1}/_{2}$ in
Wheelbase		7 ft 7$^{3}/_{4}$ in	7 ft 7$^{3}/_{4}$ in
Performance		"Motor" R/T No. 44/65	"Motor" R/T No. 50/65
Max speed			
Top gear		75.9 mph (mean)	81.9 mph (mean)
		79.7 mph (best)	84.3 mph (best)
3rd gear		65 mph	67 mph
2nd gear		40 mph	42 mph
1st gear		22 mph	25 mph
Acceleration			
0–30 mph		5.2 seconds	5.2 seconds
0–50 mph		13.3 seconds	13.1 seconds
0–60 mph		20.8 seconds	19.8 seconds
0–70 mph		37.9 seconds	32.9 seconds
		Top gear/3rd gear	Top gear/3rd gear
20–40 mph		11.7/7.3 seconds	10.5/6.9 seconds
30–50 mph		13.2/8.5 seconds	10.4/7.5 seconds
40–60 mph		16.9/12.5 seconds	13.4/10.0 seconds
50–70 mph		24.1/– seconds	18.7/– seconds
Fuel consumption		35.0 mpg (1780 miles)	28 mpg (1773 miles)

VICTOR 101, VX 4/90 FC SERIES

With three distinct model ranges giving them excellent penetration in the small, medium, and large-car sectors, Vauxhall were able to give each model a three-year run in substantially unaltered form, whilst bringing out a new model every year. For 1965 it was the Victor's turn for replacement, and the new Victor 101 FC Series duly appeared in October 1964 just in time for the Earls Court Motor Show.

On the same track and wheelbase as the outgoing FB Victor, and with substantially the same floorpan and bracing members, was a completely restyled four-door body wider by just half an inch, and longer by $1\frac{1}{2}$ inches than before. A prominent feature of this was the curvature of the sides, including the glass, which had been adopted for two important reasons; these being 4 inches more shoulder width inside the car, and a considerable increase in the bodyshell's torsional rigidity. In fact with this

design, and careful attention to detail such as the provision of box-section fore and aft roof rails above the doors, the new Victor's all-welded structure possessed some 70% greater rigidity than the preceding model, and in so doing was ranking amongst the best in this respect.

Still mindful of the corrosion problems which had afflicted their later 1950s models, Vauxhall again applied underbody sealant to both sides of the floorpan, and sprayed a similar compound into the box-section sills. Detachable splash shields, screwed into place behind the front wheels, were a neat arrangement which would stop mud and road dirt from accumulating at the rear of the front wing against the front door pillar where it does so much damage on so many cars.

Obviously then well-protected underneath, the new range also featured the new acrylic paint finish first seen on the Viva, whilst almost all of the exterior bright metal trim was in anodized aluminium. The bumper bars displayed a chromed finish, and were very effectively styled into the Victor's bodywork, but being virtually flush-fitting as they were, however, seriously limited their effectivenes as body-damage preventors in the event of even a mild collision. Indeed, actually including the side and direction indicators lamps in the front bumper itself seemed to confirm that the bumpers in this case were more decorative than anything else.

The bonnet top, hinged at its rear, was virtually as wide as the car itself, and gave good accessibility to the underbonnet components; a pity, though, that it was still not self-supporting. At the other end of the car, the equally wide boot lid was counterbalanced, and opened to reveal a very roomy and sensibly shaped compartment which was even larger than that of the previous Victor, with the increase in size being the result of rather more rear overhang. The layout here was as before, with an underslung 10 gallon fuel tank, and the spare wheel secured inside the right hand rear wing.

The four doors gave good access to a passenger compartment of adequate fore and aft room, and very generous width which would now more than justify a six-seater claim for those Victors with a bench front seat. As before, there were standard, Super, and De Luxe trim levels, with the two lower models again featuring the bench seat in the front, with the individual front seats appearing as normal equipment in the De Luxe whilst

Imaginative brochure artwork depicted the new Victor 101 to perfection. "Vauxhall engineers conquer the space problem" said the brochure caption, referring of course to the new Victor's remarkable interior roominess; but the space-travel theme for the illustrations set them off very well.

Down to earth – and looking just as good. EXE 783C is a brand-new example featuring in this Vauxhall publicity pose . . .

being optional at extra cost on the other two cars. All the seats were redesigned, with thicker squabs – of greater curvature on the individual front seats – and larger cushions giving more under-the-knees support. Trim material was PVC, with the more expensive Ambla variety of this for the De Luxe car on which the previously standard leather seating was now only to be available at extra cost. Felt pads under the floorcoverings of all the cars were in the interests of making these latest Victors quieter running than before.

A concave facia had a well-padded top, and the new two-spoked steering wheel featured padding across its centre. Rectangular instruments replaced

the former dials, and blended in well with the new design. A parcel shelf running beneath the facia had a centre compartment with a lockable sliding door on the De Luxe car.

A new heating and ventilation system had been designed, with the fresh air ventilation part of the system and its controls being standard on all models, whilst the heater unit itself remained an option except on the De Luxe car which came with the complete system as standard equipment. Air was directed into the front passenger area through central ducts, and, via ducts low down on the inside front panels at each side of the car, past the seats and into the rear compartment. With the heater unit, which was mounted centrally on the engine side of the bulkhead came two blower motors, one for each side of the car. Maximum heater output was said to be 20% greater than before, and with a wider degree of control.

Apart from a raise in compression ratio to 9.0:1 (8.5:1 previously) which increased the power output to 60 bhp at 4600 rpm, the 1594 cc engine was otherwise exactly as before. A softer rear engine-mount, a smaller diameter four-bladed fan, and an exhaust system now attached to the inner sills rather than the floorpan were all changes designed to reduce the noise and vibration entering the passenger compartment. The De Luxe Victor now also had the advantage of the VX 4/90 exhaust system with its additional box which reduced the noise on the over-run. A change was to be seen in the abandonment of the hydraulic operation for the clutch, although thankfully the new mechanical arrangements adopted consisted of rods and bell cranks, rather than the cheap cable affair which was to be seen on the Viva. The excellent three- and four-speed all synchromesh gearboxes were to be seen once again, with the three-speed unit being the standard fitment on all three Victors. The floor gearchange lever of the four-speed gearbox now had a shorter movement across the gate, and was now insulated by a rubber bush between it and the stub on which it was mounted; whilst this helped with noise suppression, it was also said to improve the feel of the gearchange. Completing the transmission came the 4.125:1 final drive assembly as on the earlier cars.

. . . whereas EAT 292C was photographed when six years old in 1971.

The standard bench front seat of the lesser models allowed comfortable three-abreast seating in the front. The heater duct which blew warm air past the front seats into the rear compartment can be seen ahead of the door.

The recirculating ball steering gear was retained, and the only changes to be seen in the suspension were that the anti-roll bar linking the independent front suspension units was stiffened up considerably by an increase of $^1/16$ inch in its diameter, whilst at the rear the usual U-bolts securing the leaf springs to the axle had given way to an arrangement in which the spring was gripped between upper and lower plates. The upper of these plates was attached to the underside of the axle casing, and with rubber insulation between the spring and each of the plates the design was effective in reducing road noise.

9 inch diameter brake drums all round, rather than the 9 inch front/8 inch rear drums of the FB series suggested improvements in braking performance, although at 102 square inches the brake lining area was still poor, and the front disc brakes of the VX 4/90 which were still to be a Victor option were without doubt a much better bet. A new feature of the all drum system was that the shoes were self-adjusting. Completing the running gear once again came the 13 inch roadwheels with 5.60 x 13 tyres.

With prices of £678, £708, and £763 for the standard, Super, and De Luxe models respectively, the new Victors were not quite so well-placed pricewise as had been the preceding FB series cars. Ford's De Luxe Corsair was still only £701, whilst BMC's Farina Austin Cambridge/Morris Oxford series were still looking good at prices between £722 and £766; and all of these included a four-speed gearbox as standard, whereas on the Vauxhalls an extra £14/10s was charged for this. In terms of performance however the four-speed Victor would generally out-accelerate these rivals, with its standstill to 60 and 70 mph times of around 17 and 27 seconds being good for this class of car, whilst its maximum speed of 83 mph was about average.

An estate car variant, and the luxury/high-performance VX 4/90 were again completing the range, with the estate car now offering really excellent carrying capacity with a full 6 feet maximum loading length. Like the previous model the saloon's rear wings were retained, with a nicely raked tailgate finishing off the neat styling of this load-carrying Victor; although of course chosen to cope with the extra loads, the bigger tyres (5.90 x 13) also improved the estate car's appearance by more effectively filling the large wheelarches. Available with both Super and De Luxe trim levels, at £779 and £859, these Victors did have to contend with such as the Hillman Super

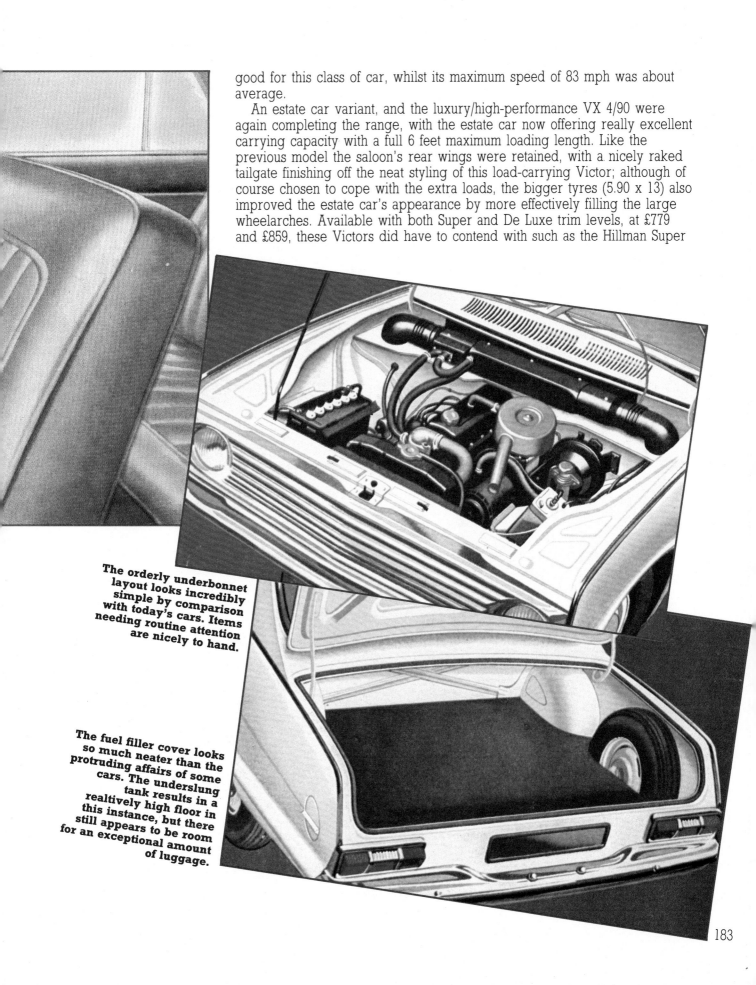

The orderly underbonnet layout looks incredibly simple by comparison with today's cars. Items needing routine attention are nicely to hand.

The fuel filler cover looks so much neater than the protruding affairs of some cars. The underslung tank results in a realtively high floor in this instance, but there still appears to be room for an exceptional amount of luggage.

Minx estate at £799, and the Morris Oxford Traveller at £839.

Topping the range once again, now at £872, the VX 4/90 offered higher performance and a greater degree of luxury than the Victors, and as before could be readily identified by its contrastingly-coloured side "flash" and exclusive grille design. Inside, the VX 4/90 trim was little different now from the De Luxe Victor, with similar Ambla upholstery, but the instrument panel

Datapanel: Vauxhall FC Series Victor 101, VX 4/90

	Victor 101	VX 4/90
Engine	4 cyl, ohv	4 cyl, ohv
Capacity	1594 cc	1594 cc
Bore	81.6 mm	81.6 mm
Stroke	76.2 mm	76.2 mm
Compression ratio	9.0:1	9.3:1
Max BHP	60 @ 4600 rpm	73.8 @ 5200 rpm
Max torque	86 lbs/ft @ 2400 rpm	98.7 lbs/ft @ 3200 rpm
Gearing	16.5 mph/1000 rpm	17.5 mph/1000 rpm
Tyres	5.60 x 13	5.60 x 13
Kerb weight	20 cwt	20^1/2 cwt
Overall length	14 ft 7 in	14 ft 7 in
Overall width	5 ft 4^1/2 in	5 ft 4^1/2 in
Wheelbase	8 ft 4 in	8 ft 4 in
Performance		
	"Motor" R/T No. 9/65 (4-speed)	"Autocar" 1st October 1965
Max speed Top gear	83.7 mph (mean) 86.1 mph (best)	93.0 mph (mean) 96.0 mph (best)
3rd gear	70 mph	70 mph
2nd gear	45 mph	45 mph
1st gear	28 mph	29 mph
Acceleration		
0–30 mph	5.2 seconds	5.0 seconds
0–50 mph	11.7 seconds	11.5 seconds
0–60 mph	17.1 seconds	16.0 seconds
0–70 mph	27.2 seconds	22.3 seconds
0–80 mph	–	34.4 seconds
	Top gear/3rd gear	Top gear/3rd gear
20–40 mph	9.8/6.4 seconds	10.3/6.6 seconds
30–50 mph	9.2/6.7 seconds	10.7/7.5 seconds
40–60 mph	11.6/9.6 seconds	11.7/9.1 seconds
50–70 mph	16.8/– seconds	13.9/11.0 seconds
60–80 mph	–/–	20.2/– seconds
Fuel consumption	23.8 mpg (1030 miles)	23.3 mpg (1068 miles)

differed in that it consisted of four circular housings, of which the speedometer and rev counter occupied the two central positions which could be viewed through the steering wheel just nicely below the arc of the full circle hornring.

The VX engine was exactly as previously, with 73.8 bhp at 5200 rpm, with the standard four-speed gearbox and 3.9:1 also being as before. A surprise, though, was the adoption of the Victor's 13 inch diameter wheels in place of the previous VX 4/90's 14 inch rims. This now lowered the gearing from 18.1 mph/1000 rpm to 17.5 mph/1000 rpm with the normal 5.60 x 13 tyres, and as the new car was weighing in almost exactly the same as before a slight improvement in acceleration and flexibility could be expected. The smaller wheels now resulted in 9 inch diameter front disc brakes in place of those previously of 10 inches, and another surprise was that the system was now by Girling rather than Lockheed as before. Self-adjusting rear drums accompanied the front disc brakes, and the system was servo assisted.

A little cleaner aerodynamically, this latest VX 4/90 would marginally outrun the preceding 1.6 litre model, reaching speeds in the 93 to 95 mph bracket, albeit with rather more commotion from under the bonnet than with the earlier higher-geared car.

Rapid brake lining wear, and too-easily induced brake fade particularly on the all-drum Victors resulted in the self-adjusting brakes giving way to a normal arrangement within a matter of months. Whilst this no doubt improved the situation considerably on the drum braked cars, a far better

Retaining the saloon's rear wing line, and tail lamp treatment, resulted in a stylish estate car version. Extending the roof colour to surround the tailgate window effectively breaks up a rather large expanse of metal, thus making the two-tone option perhaps rather more desirable than had it been applied to the roof only.

proposition on the Victors was the optional front disc brake set up complete
with the servo assistance as on the VX 4/90, and at only £15 extra if
specified on any Victor.

A Borg-Warner limited-slip differential became optional throughout the
range in May 1965, and at £9/13s/4d seemed most desirable as it did of
course offer considerably improved traction under poor conditions. This was
quickly followed by another new option on the high-performance VX 4/90 in
the form of a set of 155 x 13 Avon radial-ply tyres. These were of quite
adequate width, and improved the adhesion by comparison with the
standard 5.60 x 13 crossplies, but were unfortunately of noticeably smaller
diameter than these and therefore lowered the gearing further whilst also
looking far too small on this relatively big-bodied car.

The Powerglide two-speed automatic transmission first seen on the
six-cylinder Vauxhalls some time previously also became an option in mid
1965, adding £97 to the price of a Victor or VX 4/90 when specified. The
limited-slip differential became standard on the VX 4/90 in September 1965,
with the price adjusted accordingly, whilst remaining an option on the
lower-powered models. The De Luxe Victors now received walnut-finish
facia inserts, and all the range were now benefiting from further sound

deadening material being included during manufacture.

For 1967 the VX 4/90 featured slight trim changes including a walnut finish for its facia panels, and lower down the range the Victor Super now came with the heater unit as standard equipment. A mechanical change was a modified flywheel to absorb some out-of-balance forces which gave rise to crankshaft rumble on some, but apparently by no means all, Victor and VX engines. The entire range continued until the late summer of 1967 when they were then deleted to make way for the all-new overhead camshaft-engined Victor FD Series.

. . . whilst inside it featured its own exclusive appointments as seen here in this brochure montage.

APPENDIX: OWNERS' CLUBS

A40 Farina Club. 113 Chastilian Road, Dartford, Kent DA1 3LN.

Austin Cambridge/Westminster Car Club. Mr. P. Curtis, 63 Westbury Road, Westbury-on-Trym, Bristol. BS9 3AS.

Cambridge/Oxford Owners' Club (inc. Wolseley/Riley/MG Farina). Mr. B. Edmonds, 36 North Western Avenue, Watford. WD2 6AE.

Mini Owners' Club. 15 Birchwood Road, Lichfield. WS14 9UN.

Mini Cooper Club (inc. all Minis). Joyce Holman, 1 Weavers Cottage, Church Hill, West Hoathly, Sussex.

Mini Cooper Register (inc. all Minis). Carol Evans, 394 Gressal Lane, Tile Cross, Birmingham.

The 1100 Club (all f.w.d. 1100 models). Mr. D. Withington, 35 Stanley Street, Tunstall, Stoke-on-Trent, Staffs.

Morris Minor Owners' Club. Jane White, 127-129 Green Lane, Derby. DE1 1RZ.

Ford 105E Owners' Club. Martin Lewis, 81 Compton Road, North End, Portsmouth, Hants. PO2 0SR.

Ford Classic & Capri Owners' Club. Maureen Salmon, 58 Dewey Road, Dagenham, Essex.

Ford Consul Capri Club (inc. Classic 315). 53 Middle Street, Brockham, Surrey. RH3 7JT.

Ford Mk 111 Zephyr & Zodiac Owners' Club. Chris. Bagley, 33 Cambridge Road, Mitcham, Surrey. CR4 1DW.

Mk 1 Cortina Owners' Club. Mr. R. Raisey, 51 Studley Rise, Trowbridge, Wilts. BA14 OPD.

Ford Corsair Owners' Club. Mrs. E. Checkley, 7 Barnfield, New Malden, Surrey. KT3 5RH.

Hillman Owners' Club. P.O. Box 49, Hertford. SG14 2PG.

Rootes Easidrive Register (Minx/Gazelle/Vogue with Easidrive transmission). Mr. K. Molley, 35 Glenesk Road, London. SE9 1AG.

Singer Owners' Club. Mr. M. Way, 52 Waverley Gardens, Stamford, Lincs.

Association of Singer Car Owners. Mr. K. Hogben, 4 Ashdown Close, Gifford Park (South), Milton Keynes. MK14 5PX.

The Imp Club. Mr. B. Wright, 10 Viscount Road, Stanwell, Middlesex. TW19 7RD.

Club Triumph Ltd. Mr. M. Warren, 13 John Simpson Close, Wolston, Coventry. CV8 3HX.

Triumph Drivers Club 1985. Mr. C. Swinbourne, 10 Deerhurst Close, Newbarn, Longfield, Kent. DA3 7LL.

Triumph Sports Six Club (inc. Herald/Vitesse). Freepost, 121B St Marys Road, Market Harborough, Leics. LE16 7DT.

Triumph Sporting Owners' Club. Mr. K. James, 38 Charlton Avenue, Hyde, Cheshire.

The F-Victor Owners' Club & Register (inc. FB Series). Mr. D. Holder, 40 Gallows Hill Lane, Abbotts Langley, Watford, Herts. WD5 0DA.

Vauxhall PA/PB/PC/ E Series Owners' Club. Mr. S. Walker, 69 Framfield Road, Hanwell, London. W7 1NQ.

The Viva Owners' Club. Mr. A. Miller, The Thatches, Snetterton North End, Snetterton, Norwich. NR16 2LD.

Victor 101 FC Club. 12 Cliffe Crescent, Ellerdine, Telford, Shropshire.

Vauxhall VX 4/90 Drivers Club. 37 Masefield Crescent, Abingdon, Oxon. OX14 5PM.